WAR OF VENGEANCE

Acts of Retaliation Against Civil War POWs

Lonnie R. Speer

STACKPOLE
BOOKS

Copyright © 2002 by Stackpole Books

Published by
STACKPOLE BOOKS
5067 Ritter Road
Mechanicsburg, PA 17055
www.stackpolebooks.com

Printed in the United States of America

10 9 8 7 6 5 4 3 2 1

FIRST EDITION

Library of Congress Cataloging-in-Publication Data

Speer, Lonnie R.
    War of vengeance : acts of retaliation against Civil War POWs / Lonnie Speer.
        p. cm.
    Includes bibliographical references and index.
    ISBN 0-8117-1388-1
    1. United States—History—Civil War, 1862–1865—Prisoners and prisons. 2. Prisoners of war—Crimes against—United States—History—19th century. 3. Prisoners of war—Crimes against—Confederate States of America—History. 4. Revenge—Case studies. I. Title.

E615 .S66 2002
973.7'71—dc21
                                                                          2002020510

To Melba—
for her love, devotion, and understanding,
her constant faith, endearing praise, and gentle encouragement.

Contents

Acknowledgments

A gain, I would like to thank the many people who have helped make this book possible. With each new scholarly work, I become indebted to more and more people.

A special thanks goes to Fred Bauman and Ernest Emrich at the Library of Congress and to Maja Keech in the Photo Division of the Library of Congress for their diligent effort and sincere interest in helping me locate some elusive information in their holdings. Thanks as well go to the enthusiastic staff at the National Archives, who are as equally interested in assisting in uncovering valuable information held there; to Michael J. Winey, curator of the Carlisle Barracks U.S. Army Military History Institute at Carlisle, Pennsylvania, and his most efficient associate Randy W. Hackenburg, who are both always interested in sharing the wealth of information in their holdings; to the Wilson Library staff of the Rare Book and Manuscripts Department, Southern Historical Collection, University of North Carolina at Chapel Hill, for making their holdings available; and to Chris Montgomery, Fae Sotham, and Pat Holmes of the State Historical Society of Missouri at the University of Missouri at Columbia, for their generous and courteous assistance.

I am equally grateful for all the information and help from Carol Brentlinger and Tom Meade of Palmyra, Missouri; Gerry Vogel, reference librarian of the Sandusky, Ohio, Library; Myron E. Neal, department manager, Magazines & Newspapers, at the Public Library of Cincinnati and Hamilton County, Ohio; Joan L. Clark, head librarian of the Cleveland Public Library; and the always helpful staff at the Pack Memorial Library in Asheville, North Carolina, including their diligent associates at the Black Mountain and Swannanoa branches.

Thanks go also to Jack Mort, Leon Kirk, and Rudy Scott Nelson for the much needed, hard-to-locate information they were able to provide; to Lynn Burnett of Kentucky for the additional information she uncovered; to E. A. (Bud) Livingston of New York, Tom McCarthy of New York, Prof. William B. Jordan, Jr., of Portland, Maine, M. O. Freeman of San Jose, California, Dorris D. Beck of Sylva, North Carolina, and John H. Galbreath of Black Mountain, North Carolina, for the specialized information they provided; and my sincere appreciation to Dan Slagle of Swannanoa, North Carolina, for providing some of the most obscure firsthand accounts and documents regarding his specialized local interest.

In addition, my appreciation goes out to the following for their sincere enthusiasm and constant encouragement: My wife Melba, Mark S., Andy S., Lori Pike, Randy and Merlinda S., Glen and the late Betty S., Danny and Pam Slagle, Charles and Fran Dewberry, Evelyn Frizsell, John and Debby Burchfield, Bob and Cheryl Milner, Steve and Lenna Bucy, Virginia Bucy, J. B. Simmons, Harvey Davis, Leo and Brindia Gaines, Larry Miller, Judd Dougherty, Lonnie Johnson, James Ellerbee, Harold Cruell, Hugh and Jeanette Furan, Doug and Cindy Grimm, Len Amato, John and Amy Pavone, Rick and Jeanie Wilkerson, Karen Milton, Dr. Harold Gollberg, Gerald and Genelyn Dean, John and Jeanie Jonas, Dr. Rodolfo and Sonya Valencia, Ron and Mely Cappella, Joe and Belen Palmisano, Darel and Carol Malcolm, Connie Blalock, George Owensby, Doris Moore, Mr. and Mrs. Steve Shope, Marley Stepp, Tommy Lockhart, Andy Gwynn, Steve Teixeira, Harry Biddix, Leon Stewart, Les Whittington, Kenny McKenny, David and Beebee Watson, Dr. Robert and Pat Fulbright, Evalee Fulbright, Gary and Kay Quint, Geoff and Shelly Morrison, Dave and Kathy DeGonia, Robert Friedman, Tom VonHatten, Jim Kempf, Rich Wheeler, Rich Franz, Jim Neff, Mike Burnette, Jerry Fuller, Chris Ryans, Al Ellis, Tony Meadows, Sue McMahan, Betty Budd, June Rogers, Dorothy Marks, Jeannie and the late Wayne Beavers, Ralph and Alice Schiefelbein, Richard and Maxine Jones, Roy and Linda Greenlee, Ray and Betty Greenlee, David and Shirley Greenlee, Harold and Jacqueline Greenlee, Dale and Collette Rickert, Arletta Moore, Ed and Sue Curtis, Stan and Cathy Clardy, Col. James L. Speicher, Jim and Judy Beckner, and the Avenido family.

Special recognition also goes out to my editors Leigh Ann Berry, William C. "Jack" Davis, and Ryan Masteller of Stackpole Books who watched over, directed, and piloted this book to its final form. And I recognize, as well, Peter Rossi of Stackpole for his untiring devotion in promoting and assisting all the authors at so many special events and the giving of so much of his personal time.

My sincerest thanks go to each and every one of you who have, in your own individual ways, helped make this book a reality. Many thanks go, too, to those who have written since my last book with words of encouragement, to provide gifts of research material, or to ask a question. I have tried to answer all of you but if I have missed anyone, please forgive me.

Introduction: The Laws of War

The law of war can no more wholly dispense with retaliation than can the law of nations of which it is a branch;
yet civilized nations acknowledge retaliation as the
sternest feature of war. . . . Retaliation will therefore never
be resorted to as a measure of mere revenge but only as a
means of protective retribution. . . . Unjust or inconsider-
ate retaliation removes the belligerents farther and farther
from the mitigating rules of a regular war and by rapid
steps leads them nearer to the internecine wars of savages.

Instructions for the government of armies
of the United States in the field
By order of the Secretary of War
Approved by the President of the United States

The "laws" of war not withstanding, the American Civil War was a vicious
conflict that developed an intense hatred on both sides that degenerated
into an entirely different concept than what many historians are willing to
concede. In fact, many still maintain it was history's last "Gentleman's
War," believing that a chivalrous and cavalier attitude existed throughout
the conflict. Evidence of the opposite, however, cannot be ignored. Within

months of its beginning this conflict was anything but "civil" and conducted by anyone but "gentlemen." There is ample documentation to suggest both sides quite commonly practiced retaliatory measures against each
other for real or imagined wrongs throughout the war. It became most apparent, however, in the taking of prisoners. Using their POWs as mere
pawns, the retaliation directed against them took many forms. Mental
abuse and several degrees of physical abuse were quite often used to obtain
information, to recruit prisoners for military service, or to coerce oaths of
allegiance. Both sides scouted their military prisons in an effort to recruit
troops or to eliminate potential manpower for the enemy. When the prisoners refused to join or to take an oath of allegiance both governments
often enacted some type of reprisal against them. Sometimes this involved
rations being withheld or sometimes mental or physical abuse was used
against individuals or entire groups.[1]

To their captors these prisoners represented the embodiment of the
opposing army—a group that frustrations and anger could be vented
against on a personal level. The anger might be the result of the death of a
friend or loved one in the war, a particular battle that was lost, or the frus-
tration over the war in general. Such hostilities were not only acted out by
individuals, including prison commandants and guards, but also by the
press, the public, and, sometimes, even the governments holding them.[2]

But the most incredulous and least known aspect of this war was the
actual killing of these unarmed men for some real or imagined evil on the
battlefield or elsewhere. Sometimes it was done as soon as the POWs were
captured, right after they threw down their weapons and raised their hands
to surrender. Sometimes it happened after they were marched a short distance away from the battlefield—out of sight of the enemy—and sometimes it was done by cold-blooded executions at the prisons—weeks or
months after their capture; often chosen for death by a lottery or drawing.
Such practices—which occurred more often than the general public realizes
or many historians will accept—were often sanctioned by historically fa-
mous well-known individual commanders, by military companies, by entire armies, and by the governments themselves. In fact, the retaliation was
sometimes sanctioned at the very highest levels of authority of both sides.
Ultimately, there were times that this war was often reduced to a "war of
retaliation" with "official" threats of retaliation met with "official" threats of
counter-retaliation. Unfortunately, it was seldom conducted against the

guilty. Most often it was conducted against the innocent—those conveniently in custody who had nothing to do with the original incident.

"[T]his Government will deal out to the prisoners held by it the same treatment and the same fate as shall be experienced by those captured [by the Union]," declared Confederate president Jefferson Davis within the first week of July 1861.[3]

"If it should become necessary," declared Edwin M. Stanton, Union secretary of war, "strict retaliation will be resorted to."[4]

Union president Abraham Lincoln, who detested any kind of retaliatory measures and often went out of his way to have scheduled executions postponed or commuted whenever possible, finally conceded in mid-1863 and advised members of his cabinet, "for every soldier of the United States killed in violation of the laws of war a rebel soldier shall be executed." Afterwards, he personally authorized or approved a number of retaliation executions.[5]

"[W]e must let Mr. Lincoln understand," John Letcher, governor of Virginia, countered as he urged the Confederate secretary of war, "that for every man who shall be executed we will execute in like manner one of corresponding grade selected from the prisoners in our custody."[6]

"[T]his policy of retaliation is a two-edged sword," the *New York Times* pointed out in November 1861. "[It] opens an endless series of acts in which innocent persons on both sides must be sacrificed to public policy."[7]

Few on either side heeded the warning. In the ensuing months similar policies and practices continued on both sides until, finally, the number and frequency of such acts hit a new crescendo. Throughout 1863 and 1864 authorities of both sides constantly retaliated back and forth, confining a number of POWs in irons, reducing their rations, or executing them.

"Retaliation to be just," warned James Kent in his *Commentaries on American Law* published in the early 1800s, "ought to be confined to the guilty."[8]

"Reprisal, or the punishment of one man for the acts of another," William Edward Hall agreed in his *Treatise on International Law*, "is itself as repugnant to justice, and when hasty or excessive is so apt to increase rather than abate the irregularities of a war."[9]

There was much agreement on both sides of the Atlantic.

"Every such act," insisted one contemporary newspaper correspondent from London, criticizing the atrocities of the war in America as they gained

xiv   WAR OF VENGEANCE

international attention, "alienates thousands of friends and embitters millions of enemies. The South is made more hostile, and the restoration of the Union more hopeless."[10]

Meanwhile both the Union and Confederate governments accused each other of initiating the barbaric acts.

"In regard to retaliation," Union general Henry W. Halleck declared, "I know of no modern authority which justifies it, except in the extreme case of a war with an uncivilized foe which has himself first established such a barbarous rule."[11]

"The course which the Confederate Government has pursued," argued Robert Ould, Confederate agent for exchange, "was the result of a firm conviction on its part that it was bound by the highest obligations of duty to its own citizens to adopt such just measures of retribution and retaliation as seemed adequate to meet the injustice of [its enemy]."[12]

Throughout the conflict Northern and Southern newspapers deepened the controversy and aroused public indignation over such executions. While some citizens were appalled, others demanded further retaliation. What had begun as official threats between the two governments quickly degenerated into actual deeds on the field and continued throughout the war. For some commanders of both sides the retaliation seemed to border on the concept of systematic murder.

"[They] shall be treated as traitors and slain wherever found," threatened Col. Charles R. Jennison, 7th Kansas Cavalry, in November 1861, in his proclamation to the people of Missouri's border counties who might be taken prisoner as Southern sympathizers and who refused to surrender their arms and sign deeds of forfeiture to their property.[13]

"Three men . . . within four hours after their arrival were carried from the prison and hung," declared Confederate colonel John D. Morris, confined as a POW at Lexington, Kentucky, "and this thing went on until twenty-eight of our number, almost invariably Confederate soldiers, had fallen victims to this unheard-of barbarity. . . . These men were not tried before a military commission or court-martial. They were simply selected by the provost-marshal [Capt. Richard Vance], as it seemed to me, without any reference to the guilt or innocence of the parties, just as a butcher would go into a slaughter pen and select at his will the beeves or the sheep or the hogs which he might wish to destroy."[14]

*The usual result of guerilla warfare as practiced in Missouri, Tennessee,
Kentucky, and North Carolina during the Civil War.* STATE HISTORICAL SOCIETY OF
MISSOURI, COLUMBIA

But similar atrocities were carried out by more widely known commanders as well.

"General, I know that we have orders from you to take no prisoners,"
one provost-marshal worried in his dispatch to Union general John M.
Schofield, "[but] without judge or jury court-martial or any form of trial
. . . [they are to be] mercilessly murdered. To be done in such a manner is
uncivilized and unsoldierlike."[15]

"When any of [John S.] Mosby's men are caught," Union Lt. Gen.
Ulysses S. Grant ordered Maj. Gen. Philip H. Sheridan in August 1864,
"hang them without trial."[16] And Sheridan did. "We hung one and shot six
of his men yesterday," he reported a few days later.[17]

Even Maj. Gen. William Tecumseh Sherman went on record indicating he believed his side was above the law in its dealings with the Confederates. "The Government of the United States," he said, "[has] any and all
rights which they choose to enforce in war—to take their lives, their homes,
their lands, their everything—because . . . war is simply power unrestrained
by constitution or compact. . . . To the petulant and persistent secessionists,
why, death is mercy, and the quicker he or she is disposed of the better."[18]

A Harper's Weekly *depiction of retaliation on wounded POW's following a battle.*

As many of these statements would imply, there is also overwhelming evidence to suggest there were men in the Union army who could very well have been prosecuted as war criminals by the Confederates, had the South won the war. But with victory, of course, the atrocities committed by Union commanders went ignored.

But needless to say, just as many atrocity statements can be attributed to commanders of the Confederate forces.

Like President Lincoln, Confederate general Robert E. Lee at first wanted no part in such barbaric proceedings. "[T]he system of retaliation, if commenced, will not be on an equal basis," he warned Jefferson Davis as late as June 1863. "Besides, I am not in favor of retaliation excepting in very extreme cases, and I think it would be better for us to suffer, and be right in our own eyes and in the eyes of the world."[19]

But soon after that declaration, Lee's son was captured and President Lincoln, himself, ordered his execution in retaliation for another that was scheduled in Richmond. Finally, by November 1864, General Lee had seen all the "extreme cases" he needed to see and finally declared, "I have directed

Colonel Mosby to hang an equal number of [George A.] Custer's men in retaliation for those executed by him."[20]

Numerous examples of retaliation on the Civil War's POWs are available. They occurred throughout the war, in both theaters, on both sides, and in nearly every state that had a battle or skirmish. It would require years of research to reveal every incident and eventually such accounts would fill as many volumes as the Official Records, themselves. Therefore, the following serve only as the most notorious, most well-documented examples in the war of vengeance.

Chapter 1

"It's Me You Want"

JAMES WILSON

On October 3, 1864, James Wilson and a small group of other captured Union soldiers slowly trudged along an old dirt road under escort of a mounted Confederate cavalry guard. According to later testimony, it was a typical early-autumn day in southeast Missouri. It had become stifling hot and extremely humid and the captives had began to suffer and sweat profusely. Their dark blue wool uniforms, soaked with perspiration and some even caked with dirt and dried blood, had become unbearably heavy and uncomfortable under the hot noonday sun as their captors continued to deny them rest or water during their long trek in the dust and heat.[1]

According to that same testimony, thirty-year-old James Wilson, a major in the 3rd Missouri (Union) State Militia Cavalry, was ashamed and angry that he and some of his troops had been captured. They had fought bravely and effectively against Gen. Sterling Price's rabble of Confederate forces at Pilot Knob on September 27, and although the Union forces had been heavily outnumbered, they had successfully repelled Price's desperate assault on Fort Davidson. Still, the Union's triumph had not been successful for Wilson and some of his men. During the battle Major Wilson had held the skirmish line's left flank, located on Pilot Knob hill, with about 200 men, dismounted and deployed. Although Wilson was suffering from a slight head wound that had been hemorrhaging badly from a skirmish the day before, he had been determined it wouldn't keep him out of his

Maj. James Wilson, 3rd Missouri State Militia, executed as a POW on October 3, 1864. As it appeared in Cyrus A. Peterson's *Narrative of the Capture and Murder of Major James Wilson,* 1906

saddle or off the battlefield. Just dismounted, he began firing with one of his three revolvers while directing his men higher up on the hill when Confederate major general James Fagan's division swept over Pilot Knob and dislodged Wilson and his men, capturing some of them.[2]

According to witnesses, as senior officer in this group of captives Wilson felt responsible for the troops' welfare but, since their capture, there had been nothing he could do to help them. He and the others had languished for several days in a prison corral erected by the enemy behind the lines near where General Price had established his headquarters at Arcadia, Missouri. After a number of captives had been gathered they were force-marched out of the area. At the time, the POWs assumed they were enroute to an established jail or perhaps to a railhead where they would eventually be transported to an established military prison, as was the general procedure, where many other prisoners of war, like themselves, were being held.[3]

En route to their unknown destination, Wilson and the others, suffering from heat, fatigue, and hunger, were kicked and prodded all along the way, compelled to march in formation, and to keep pace with their horse-mounted guard escort. Up to this time they had covered a distance of seventy miles in five days during which they had waded small streams, large streams, and the Meramec River and some of its tributaries. Each time that darkness had overtaken them, they were obliged to sleep upon the bare ground at the side of the road, surrounded by a guard line. Some of the more fortunate prisoners still had their blankets to use but most of these men, like Wilson, lacked them.

As the procession continued, eighteen-year-old William Axford of Company H, 3rd Missouri State Militia, also one of the prisoners being herded along the road, later recounted having looked around at the faces of his comrades on either side of him, searching for some indication of their thoughts. He, himself, was scared, that much he knew, but he couldn't distinguish what anyone else was thinking because, without exception, their fatigued faces showed no emotion. Those he could see wore a dejected look as they stared down toward the ground watching their own feet as they moved along the road. Even among his own friends and fellow soldiers, Axford had thought to himself, he felt abandoned and all alone at the time. Briefly he thought about his fate and how if he had only headed in another direction after being routed from his hillside position on Pilot Knob, maybe he wouldn't have been captured with Major Wilson and the others.[4]

The other members of the 3rd Missouri regiment in this group of captives included John Holabaugh of Company K, captured along with Major Wilson and Private Axford; Cpl. William W. Gourley, a twenty-three-year-old who had been farming in Lincoln County, Missouri, before the war; William C. Grotts, William Skaggs, and John W. Shew, all of Company I who were captured together at another location; and Hiram Berry and Oscar O. Gilbert, of Company H.

Nearly all of these men had been farmers in Lincoln or Pike County, Missouri. If anything, they considered themselves Union moderates. They were neither antislavery zealots nor proslavery. They had no feelings about the subject either way. They simply wished to keep peace within the state and to protect it against Confederate interests so they could continue their own lives. Their military experience had been confined mostly to their home counties until General Price invaded Missouri in September with the intent of taking St. Louis. Immediately, this group and many like them were transferred to what was known as the "Secesh Country" of Southeast Missouri to repel those Confederate forces.[5]

Also in this group of captives was thirty-two-year-old Franz Dinger, a friend of Wilson's and captain of Company E, 47th Missouri Volunteer Infantry, who was captured with a number of his men after being wounded.

"We were treated very badly during this march," Dinger would later complain. Nor was he satisfied with the nourishment provided for such a trip. "We only had a little meal; very poor beef, and nothing to cook it in."

Unfortunately, the callous treatment these Missouri prisoners received was quite typical of what others experienced, both North and South, in many parts of the country. Although these particular men had no way of knowing it, by October 1864, the Confederacy held nearly 32,000 prisoners of war at various locations across the nation while the Union held nearly 52,000. In nearly every case, according to many individual accounts, they had all suffered, to one extent or another, similar treatment en route to the prisons.

As their journey continued, Wilson and the other prisoners remained silent. Each of their faces reflected some degree of indifference, resignation, or deep thought. Many were consumed with thoughts of their families or loved ones back home while others were concerned with what loomed ahead. The only sounds heard were the rustle of clothing, the squeak of saddle leather, and the occasional bark of demands from the guard as the procession moved down the road. It wasn't long, though, before their quiet thoughts were rudely interrupted.

"Halt!" commanded Lt. Col. John T. Crisp, the Confederate officer in charge of the prisoners, as he rode along the right flank of the procession. By this time the group was about ten miles south of Union, Missouri, in Franklin County.

As the captives stood on the road, facing north, they could hear the pounding of horses' hooves approaching from the south, a short distance behind them. Within moments a small band of riders rode up to the procession and quickly reined to a halt, stirring up a cloud of dust. Slowly, the lead rider rode past the prisoners and drew up close to Crisp; they began to talk quietly. Some of the prisoners recognized this new arrival as Col. Tim Reves, a guerrilla leader attached to Fagan's division. Crisp and Reves reined their horses off to one side and rode a few yards away from the group to continue their conversation in low voices.

"Line up, single file!" Crisp ordered as he rode slowly back toward the group.

The prisoners reluctantly fell into line along the center of the road as Reves slowly rode up and down the column looking over the prisoners as he passed. Upon arriving at the end of the line, he turned his horse and rode slowly past the prisoners again, glaring into their eyes and then looking over their uniforms one by one.

"Soldier, what's your name?" Reves demanded upon noticing the shoulder strap insignias on the major's jacket.

"James Wilson," came the reply.

"What regiment?" Reves shot back.

Proudly and defiantly, Wilson replied: "The [3rd] Missouri Cavalry State Militia."

"Step forward!" Reves demanded.

Wilson took two steps forward and watched as Reves continued riding down the line.

"What's your regiment?" Reves demanded of another.

"Third Missouri State Militia," answered Cpl. William Gourley.

"Step forward!" Reves again demanded and continued down the line.

Although no one seemed to know much about Reves, he appeared to be in his mid- to late thirties and, with his thick black beard, dark piercing eyes and large build, he was an imposing and intimidating figure as he sat on horseback nearly six feet above the prisoners, glaring down at them.

Upon reaching the middle of the line, Reves again turned his horse and halted, facing the prisoners. Slowly and deliberately he leaned forward in his saddle and, resting his arms across the pommel, ordered the prisoners to call out their regiments in succession.

As they did, each prisoner giving the "[3rd] Missouri State Militia" was ordered to step forward. These included William Grotts, William Skaggs, John Shew, and John Holabaugh. One prisoner, a young man of eighteen to nineteen years of age wearing the insignia of an artillery bugler and believing members of the 3rd Regiment were possibly being singled out for parole, lied and claimed to be a member of "Company H, [3rd] Missouri State Militia." To this day, his true identity is unknown. He, too, was told to step forward.

As they continued down the line and each prisoner called out his regiment, Hiram Berry and Oscar Gilbert, near the center, hastily agreed to give a different command.

"Seventeenth Illinois Cavalry," each of them said as their turn came.

Upon hearing this, William Axford, farther down the line, began to panic. "I don't like this," he muttered to the prisoner on his right. "They're singling out members of the [3rd]! What should I do?"

"Give the same regiment and company I do," the prisoner whispered out the side of his mouth as he continued facing forward.

"Company B, [14th] Iowa Infantry," the prisoner answered as his turn came.

"Company B, [14th] Iowa Infantry," Axford repeated and was relieved when Reves gave no response.

Upon hearing some of his troops give different regiments, Wilson began to sense what might be happening and became concerned about those who hadn't. "It's me you want," Wilson called out as he looked down the line at Reves. "Have the others step back in line."

"I will do no such thing, Major!" Reves blurted as he glared back at Wilson. "Now stand there and shut up!" Turning toward one of his troops, Reves then ordered: "Put a double guard on that damn major!"

After the last prisoner in line called out his regiment, Reves's men directed their horses into the lead and flanking positions around the seven who had been separated from the others, doubling up around Wilson.

Crisp then rode up to the remaining prisoners and released them on parole after they took an oath never to bear arms against the Confederacy again and after they promised to leave on a northerly route out of the area. After signing a roll, the parolees quickly departed.

"Lead 'em off!" Reves called out when the other prisoners were out of sight and Crisp had begun to lead his men out of the area in another direction.

As the Major and the six additional prisoners passed by, being led off in a southwest direction, Reves glared at Wilson and then pulled his horse in behind the group, taking up the rear position to follow them out across the flatland toward a small ridge.

Under different circumstances Reves might have admired the major. Wilson was, after all, a dashing example of a cavalry officer, being clean-cut with jet-black hair brushed to one side and a well-trimmed beard and mustache that made him look quite distinguished; as a fellow officer, he was just as admirable. Wilson was highly regarded by his troops and had developed a deep camaraderie with them. According to those who knew him,

Wilson was the kind of officer who never expected his men to do what he wouldn't do himself.[6]

But for now, Reves apparently entertained no such thoughts. Admirable foe or not, Reves had lost seven men of his command during all the skirmishing around Pilot Knob and, by all accounts, he intended to even the score.

As the group crossed over the ridge and approached a stand of trees boarding a small stream, prisoners Gourley, Grotts, Skaggs, Shew, and Holabaugh probably couldn't help but think about their families at home. Perhaps they were wishing to be back on their farms or wondering how long it would be before they got to see their families again. Whatever they were thinking, their thoughts were quickly interrupted.

"Halt!" Reves ordered.

As the prisoners stood there, next to a ravine that led down toward the creek, they could hear their rider-escort dismounting.

"About face!" Reves called out.

As the prisoners turned, for just one split second they probably saw the gaping ends of the gun barrels. Whatever they saw, in that instant after they turned around it was over. As the gunshots echoed down through the timber and across the creek, seven bodies crumpled like rag dolls and collapsed in a heap along the ground. One soldier ran over and shot Wilson's prone body twice more in the head.[7]

Calmly, the soldiers climbed back onto their horses and rode off over the ridge, out of sight.

Three weeks later, as newspapers from St. Louis to New York City ran banner headlines proclaiming that Grant and Lee had reached a mutual arrangement to alleviate the sufferings of prisoners of war, six Confederate prisoners were led out of St. Louis's Gratiot Street Military Prison to a waiting covered wagon. Under escort of a detachment of the 10th Kansas Infantry, the prisoners were taken to a site designated as Fort No. 4 near Jefferson and Ann Avenue, a short distance south of Lafayette Park. There, six upright posts, arranged in a north-south row, had been set in the ground on the west side of the compound. Each post had a seat attached. The prisoners were led to their places, tied into position, and blindfolded.[8]

Men of religion spoke to these men, after which a death sentence was read.

One prisoner, Charles W. Mineckin, asked to speak and was allowed. "I have been a Confederate soldier for four years," he said, "and have served my country faithfully. I am now to be shot for what other men have done, that I had no hand in, and know nothing about."[9]

Ten paces away stood a firing squad. Made up of the 10th Kansas and the 41st Missouri Regiments, the men appeared fidgety and some even reluctant to take aim. Their commanding officer approached and demanded they perform their duty no matter how disagreeable. Slowly, the soldiers lifted their weapons and took aim at the figures sitting against the pine posts.

It was three o'clock, Saturday afternoon, October 29, 1864. Earlier that morning these condemned men were told for the first time that they would be executed later in the day. When they asked why, they were told it was in retaliation for the death of Maj. James Wilson. None of these men understood that answer.[10]

Four days previously, on October 25, Federal authorities stationed in St. Louis were summoned to what was known as the old Jefferson farm, fifteen miles southwest of Washington, Missouri, about forty-five miles west of St. Louis. There, hogs had uncovered several human bodies, partially clad in Union uniforms, from some shallow graves.

When Col. G. Harry Stone, Gen. Edward C. Pike's chief of staff, 1st Military District, Missouri Enrolled Militia, arrived on the scene, he and his men identified one body from the trimmings of a jacket as being an artillery bugler, estimated to be eighteen to nineteen years old, belonging to Co. K, 3rd Regiment, Missouri State Militia.

Another body was identified as that of Sgt. John W. Shew, Co. I "Red Rovers," 3rd Missouri State Militia Cavalry. Before the war, Shew had been a farmer in Pike County, Missouri. He later served in Stone's command and was known by him personally.[11]

A third body was identified as Pvt. William C. Grotts, same company, same regiment. Grotts was originally from Pike County, Illinois, and had enlisted on April 7, 1863, at Louisiana, Missouri. He was more commonly known to his friends as "Red" because of his bright red hair.[12]

A fourth body was identified as Pvt. William Skaggs, but two other bodies were so badly eaten by hogs, they could not be identified. A seventh body, however, had been recognized by Stone and the others as soon as they had arrived on the scene. It was Maj. James Wilson, who had been shot several times. Closer examination revealed that Wilson had sustained two shots to the right side of the breast, one at close range to the back of the head, and another to the head behind the left ear. There was no doubt, Wilson and the others had been executed. Immediately, the findings were relayed to Department Headquarters in St. Louis.[13]

On October 28 an inquiry was held in that city and testimony was taken of those who had been part of the original capture or had witnessed the latest scene and identified the bodies.[14]

"On the 27th of September, at one o'clock P.M., I was ordered to report to Major Wilson at Pilot Knob at the railroad depot," recalled thirty-three-year-old Franz Dinger, captain of Co. E, 47th Infantry, Missouri Volunteers, during his testimony relating the events that led up to the fateful capture.

> I was stationed there with my company about half an hour when Major Wilson ordered me to the Pilot Knob hill. I stayed there about five minutes, when Major Wilson, with twenty-six dismounted cavalry, arrived. . . . He ordered me to go up higher, . . . about 300 yards from where I was, and then ordered his men still higher, as skirmishers. He remained with me and my company. In about an hour and a half we were attacked by the enemy on all sides, with the exception of the side toward Fort Davidson, and we took up our position in a hollow of the road leading to the pinnacle of the Knob. We then fired about fourteen rounds, but finding the return fire too strong for us, I ordered the men to fall back slowly to the foot of the hill and to keep firing . . . Major Wilson had three revolvers and kept firing . . . at the advancing enemy. When we got to the foot of the hill, we fired four more rounds but the enemy's fire was so strong we could not make a stand, so I ordered the men to fall back behind [a nearby] steam mill. About fifteen of the men did so, but the rest scattered. Major Wilson, myself, and five men were off at the mill and were taken prisoners.

Dinger went on to report that the following morning they were taken to a prison corral outside Arcadia, Missouri, where more prisoners were gathered and then marched to the rear of Price's army. From there they were force-marched through several more towns to Union, Missouri.

"We had no blankets or covering and were compelled to sleep on the ground just as we were," Dinger went on to say. "At Union, ten miles west of that place, on October 3, we were called into line by a man who was called Inspector General, a Colonel, I believe, and he rode up and down the line asking where we were captured and what our names were. After riding up and down two or three times he picked out six men of Major Wilson's regiment."

Captain Dinger further testified that as he and others were released, Wilson and the six troops were held under guard awaiting the arrival of Maj. Tim Reves and that was the last he ever saw of them.

When the authorities were satisfied that the newly discovered bodies were, indeed, those of Wilson and his men, the rolls of Gratiot Street Prison were closely reviewed and six men where chosen to suffer retaliatory measures.

The first placed on the death list was James W. Gates, a twenty-one-year-old private in Co. M, 3rd Missouri Cavalry, C.S.A., who had been captured in Jasper County, Missouri, on October 10, 1864. He had been sworn into the Confederate service in Barry County, Missouri, on September 13, 1862. Gates had fought against the Union in battles at Helena, Pine Bluff, Osceola, and Prairie Des Arc, Arkansas, and at Huntsville, Missouri.

Second on the list was Asa V. Ladd, a thirty-four-year-old farmer from Stoddard County, Missouri. Ladd had been captured October 16, 1864, while serving as a private in Jackson's Co. A, 4th (Burbridge's) Missouri Cavalry, sworn into the Confederate service March 16, 1861. Ladd had just arrived at Gratiot Street Prison the day that Wilson's body was discovered. He had been involved in a number of skirmishes but no general engagements. Ladd was married with four children.

Next was Charles W. Mineckin, aged twenty-two, from Independence County, Arkansas. Mineckin was captured near Jefferson City, Missouri, on October 8, 1864, and had been in Confederate service since June 10, 1861. He had fought under Gens. Ben McCulloch, Thomas Churchill, Evander McNair, Dandridge McRae, John Adams, and James Fagan's division of Price's army. He had been in battles at Oak Hill, Pea Ridge, and

Murfreesboro and had been in camp with his command in the states of Mississippi, Tennessee, Kentucky, Georgia, Alabama, Florida, North and South Carolina, Arkansas, and Missouri.

Fourth on the death list was John Nicholds of Co. G, 2nd Missouri Cavalry, C.S.A. Nicholds was a twenty-one-year-old Cass County, Missouri, resident. He had been in the service of the Confederate army since August 12, 1862, and was captured October 7, 1864. Nicholds had served under Thomas Hindman, Sterling Price, and Joseph Shelby and fought in battles at Lone Jack, Newtonia, Cans Hill, Wilson's Creek, and Cape Girardeau, Missouri.

The fifth man chosen was John N. Ferguson, a private in Co. A, Crabtree's Regiment, Arkansas Cavalry. Ferguson was twenty-three and lived in Izard County, Arkansas. He was captured near Jefferson City, Missouri, on October 8, 1864. Ferguson had joined the Confederate army November 18, 1863, and had served under Generals Fagan and McRae but had been in no engagements. He had been sick most of the time and had done duty as a teamster. He had no wife, no children, and no relatives in the Confederate service.

The last name chosen was Harvey H. Blackburn, the oldest of the six. Blackburn was forty-seven and had been a farmer in Independence, Arkansas. He was married with two children and had served in the Confederate army since April 1, 1861. He, too, was captured near Jefferson City on October 8, 1864. Blackburn had done service under McRae in the battles of Wilson's Creek, Richmond (Kentucky), Shiloh, Perryville, Murfreesboro, and Pilot Knob, Missouri. He came up to Missouri with Price, in Fagan's brigade, and was at the fight at Pilot Knob on September 27, when Wilson was captured.

With their list complete, the authorities retired for the night.

At dawn the next morning, October 29, the six prisoners were informed of their fate. Most acted indifferently, apparently realizing there was no use in arguing.

Several hours passed. Father Ward of the Catholic church and Rev. Philip McKim of the Episcopal church spent the morning with the condemned. Authorities returned to the prison just before noon and announced they had reconsidered regarding one prisoner. Since Ferguson, they said, had served such a short time as a soldier and most of his service as a teamster, his name would be stricken from the death roll and the name

George F. Bunch, Co. B, 3rd Missouri Rebel Cavalry, would be substituted instead.

Ferguson collapsed to the floor and wept for joy. Bunch was stunned with disbelief.

At 2:00 P.M. the prisoners were escorted to the waiting wagon and transported to the execution site. They arrived at the west side of the fort at 2:40. Asa Ladd was led to the northernmost post, placed in the seat, facing west, and tied into place. George Nicholds was next and Harvey Blackburn next to him. George Bunch was placed against the next post, with Charles Mineckin on his left and James Gates against the southernmost post.

Prayers were said. Blindfolds were applied.

As Nicholds's eyes were covered, he asked if there was any hope of postponement. He was assured there was none. "O-o-oh," he moaned, "think of the news that will go to my father and mother!"

Tears streamed down beneath several blindfolds. Each man, however, remained calm. There was no pleading—apparently they accepted that their fate had been sealed.

Lt. Col. Gustauve Heimrichs of the 41st Missouri Infantry and commandant of St. Louis's military prisons, stepped forward and read the death warrant to the condemned men.

Mineckin was allowed to make his statement and concluded by saying, "Boys, when ya kill me, kill me dead!"

The firing squad became fidgety. Sternly, Capt. Robert Jones ordered them to do their duty. They took aim.

It was 3:00 P.M.

For a brief moment there was complete silence. A crowd of several hundred spectators seemed to hold their breath in unison. Within a moment, though, the silence was broken by one loud, commanding voice: "Rea-a-dy! . . . Ai-i-m! . . ."

Upon command, thirty-six Union soldiers fired simultaneously. Five bodies immediately pitched to the left and slumped forward. The sixth soldier, Blackburn, fought for life a few seconds more. Within five minutes, all were dead. Slowly, the crowd dispersed. The bodies were cut loose and turned over to coroner John Smithers to be carted away for burial.

The ordeal, though, wasn't over yet. Within a few days a major, Enoch O. Wolf of Ford's Confederate regiment, fell into Union hands. As soon as the capture was made public, General Rosecrans issued an order to execute

Wolf on November 11 in retaliation for Major Wilson's death. Rev. Philip M. McKim, a Mason, and other masons of St. Louis learned that Wolf, too, was a mason and pled for a fourteen-day postponement. On the same day, Pres. Abraham Lincoln sent a dispatch to Gen. Rosecrans: "Suspend execution in the case of Major Wolf until further orders, and meanwhile report to me in this case."[15]

Perhaps Lincoln had had enough of these retaliatory executions by this time. Whatever the case, on December 9, 1864, Maj. Gen. Grenville Dodge replaced Rosecrans in command of the Department of the Missouri and the execution of Wolf was never carried out. In February 1865, he was transferred out to the Johnson's Island Military Prison in Ohio to await the end of the war.

Chapter 2

"Brought Down to the Level of a Skulking, Cowardly Pirate"

MICHAEL CORCORAN

Although the Union government's officially sanctioned execution of prisoners in St. Louis was the first actually carried out, it was not the first incident where both governments officially threatened such action. That occurred in the earliest days of the war in what became known as the infamous "Corcoran incident."

It seemed Michael Corcoran had always led a precarious and turbulent life. Born in Ireland in 1827, he was the son of a British Army captain. By the age of nineteen he had received a commission in the Irish Constabulary but resigned three years later in protest over British policy there and emigrated to the United States. Settling in New York City, he held various clerical jobs, eventually gained wealth as the proprietor of the Hibernia Hotel, and became active in the New York militia. In 1859 he was appointed colonel of the militia's 69th (Irish) Regiment. Within months of that appointment, and still very anti-British, he flatly refused to order out his regiment for a parade honoring the visiting Prince Albert of Wales and found himself held for court-martial. Because of the immense publicity generated by the incident, he also found himself a celebrity among the city's Irish. Luckily, for him at least, charges were dropped as soon as war broke out with the South because he was seen as indispensable in raising Irish volun-

*Col. Michael Corcoran, one of the
earliest and most controversial POW
"pawns" used for retaliation during
the Civil War.* LIBRARY OF CONGRESS

teers. He soon received the commission of colonel in the 69th New York
Militia in Federal service and led that regiment into the engagement that
would become known as first Bull Run.

Early Sunday, July 21, 1861, Col. Michael Corcoran was leading his
troops into the battle, charging up the north slope of Henry Hill, and was
repulsed twice by withering musket and rifle fire. As the morning continued, the Federal line became increasingly jumbled and confused until
Union forces were finally routed by the Confederate army. Corcoran's 69th
New York eventually served as rear guard to the resulting Federal with-
drawal and during that action Corcoran was wounded.[1]

> My regiment came off the field in admirable order . . . on
> the road to Centreville, . . . where I . . . await[ed] orders
> for future action, knowing that our artillery would need
> protection in returning. Two regiments that . . . were re-
> turning in disorder hung on my flank and when the
> [Confederate] cavalry advanc[ed] toward us, these regi-
> ments broke precipitately through my lines, throwing us
> into disorder. I dismounted and crossed a rail fence . . .

and called on the men to rally around the flag but just at this moment a discharge of carbines from the pursuing cavalry and our own artillery drowned out my voice and destroyed all my efforts to muster the men. I had only nine men who heard me and halted and those, with two officers and myself, were immediately surrounded and taken to Manassas that night.

Corcoran himself, in a book he published a year later, represented himself as a "hero," in the Bull Run battle and the subsequent retreating action—an uncontested boast eagerly accepted by the New York City Irish back home. According to R. T. Simpson, Co. H, 4th Alabama Regiment, who was there, however, William Oakley of that regiment was laying in a pine thicket at the base of Matthews Hill near where Union forces began retreating and saw the approach of a lone horseman passing near. As the rider got closer, Oakley jumped out, directing his rifle at the horseman and demanded his surrender. Oakley retained the man's saber and horse and after turning him over to authorities, learned it was Colonel Corcoran.[2]

Whatever the true facts are, all the captured Union soldiers, about forty officers, including Corcoran, and 900 enlisted men, were gathered up around the battlefield area, assembled into groups at various points, and force-marched to the nearby village of Manassas, a distance of about seven miles. Arriving at nine o'clock in the evening, the POWs were herded into an open lot, halted, searched again, and directed into a barn, which was surrounded with a line of guards.

"About the time of their arrival," noted one witness, "it began to rain, and in that place, without lights and unable to distinguish one from another, upon the floor covered with filth, without blankets or covering, officers of every grade passed the night."[3]

At ten o'clock the following morning Maj. John B. Prados, 8th Louisiana Volunteer Regiment, entered the barn and, ordering the officers to fall into double file according to their ranks, marched them out of the shelter.

"They were taken through the rain and mud," according to one onlooker, "to the Virginia Central Railroad where trains were soon to depart for Richmond."[4]

The prisoners were loaded into boxcars and remained therein confined while it rained throughout the day. In the meantime, additional prisoners, about 400 more privates, including many sick and wounded, were brought into town and loaded onto the cars. The train finally pulled out of Manassas Junction at four o'clock that evening. Accompanied by about 150 Confederate guards, the train came to a halt a few hours later at Gordonsville and rations were distributed. Once completed, the train continued onto Richmond, arriving at nine o'clock the following evening, July 23.

"It was a bright moonlit night," reported an eyewitness, "and after waiting at the station for an hour, they were marched through the streets, a distance of a mile, to a large brick building on the corner of Main and 25th streets."[5]

The building, a three-story structure, was the former John L. Ligon and Sons Tobacco Warehouse and Factory, which had been recently impressed by the Confederate government and converted into a military prison. The prisoners were led to the second and third floors for confinement causing this number of men to be so crowded together that there was hardly room to lie down.

"Next morning they arose at an early hour," the witness continued, "and were served to a breakfast of dry bread, boiled beef and coffee."[6]

Brig. Gen. John H. Winder, Richmond's Confederate provost marshal placed in charge of the POWs, visited the prisoners that first morning and apologized for the crowded conditions. Winder admitted Confederate authorities had not anticipated such a large gathering of captives. He assured the Federal officers the building next door had been confiscated for prison use and was being readied for them.

Good to his word, that afternoon all Federal officers and captured civilians were separated from the enlisted men and moved to less-crowded quarters next door. This building was originally known as Howard's Tobacco Factory but because it was attached to the Ligon's building, the entire complex became known as Ligon's Military Prison. In immediate charge of these facilities was Lt. David H. Todd, half-brother to Abraham Lincoln's wife Mary, and Sgt. Henry Wirz, who would later become associated with the Southern prison at Andersonville, Georgia.

The first nonjail structures used in Richmond to hold prisoners, the Ligon and Howard factories consisted of rooms 75 by 30 feet. The ground floors of each building had barred windows and several rows of tobacco presses that occupied about half of the floor space. The upper floor windows were unbarred but, by prison rules, the POWs were prohibited from standing near them under penalty of death by shooting.

Although the prisoners were locked into the buildings at night, conditions were more lax during the daytime hours.

"Some of the Union troops were paid off just before the battle," advised J. Lane Fitts, Co. B, 2nd New Hampshire Volunteers, "and there was probably between five hundred and one thousand dollars in gold among the prisoners. The gold the Confederates were quite willing to take, and so one man from each room was allowed to go out into the city with a guard, and buy for the rest of the men in his room. After our gold was gone, we sold one article after another to the guards."[7]

In addition, the city's blacks were allowed to go into the officers' quarters to take orders from the men and return at will with the deliveries. A number of the officers, including Michael Corcoran, even had their own body servants incarcerated with them and they were allowed to go into town unguarded to make purchases of food and other necessities for their masters.[8]

The Union POWs continued to endure under these circumstances throughout the following weeks. The captives slept on the floor—on blankets if they had them or on loose straw if they didn't—and ate their rations with their fingers. And from the first day of their arrival they remained a curiosity among the city's citizens while at least two of them gained celebrity status.

"[Cong. Alfred Ely of Rochester] and Col. Corcoran, of the Sixty-ninth New York State Regiment, have been the subjects of great attraction," advised prisoner A. H. Morrill, 13th New York Regiment. "The incessant visitation was kept up until it became a burden instead of a pleasure [and eventually was] curtailed by order of Gen. Winder, in charge of the post."[9]

As the weeks passed, conditions for the prisoners became worse and worse as more and more captives were brought into the city. A number of additional buildings were confiscated and converted to prison use but the prison rooms continued to become more crowded. Sanitation worsened, and rations had to be reduced to accommodate the ever-increasing numbers. With the harsher conditions, Congressman Ely and Colonel Corcoran began to complain loudly about the overall treatment of the prisoners.

They filed a number of petitions with the Confederate authorities and wrote letters to various newspapers. Still, conditions failed to improve.

"Some of us were sick with diarrhea," complained prisoner Fitts, "and as only two were allowed to go out in charge of a guard at a time, the line of men waiting for the privilege was, in the daytime, from twelve to twenty-five long. Money was very scarce among us, but I have known twenty-five cents to be offered and refused for a position in the line near the door."[10]

While conditions continued to worsen, Congressman Ely became quietly incensed and began to write letters to Confederate authorities and to the local newspapers while Colonel Corcoran became downright insolent and belligerent to the guards.

"[W]e already began to feel the irksomeness of our imprisonment, and longed to return to our active duties," declared Corcoran. "Sometimes those Confederate officers under whose charge we were, used to wreak their malice upon us in ways which were as contemptible as they were galling."[11]

The Confederate authorities considered the outspoken and rebellious Corcoran the main instigator of the developing insurgency among the prisoners. One local newspaper even reported that Colonel Corcoran had been placed in irons for refusing to reply when his name was called during a morning roll call.

"Not only was this entirely untrue," claimed Corcoran, "but there never was the slightest foundation for it."[12]

Still, Michael Corcoran always seemed involved with any conflict or controversy within the prison.

"[W]anton and useless brutality excited my indignation so much, that, when General Winder next paid us a visit . . . [I complained]," he admitted, "[and] Mr. Ely drew up a petition to President Lincoln, stating our condition and our place of incarceration, and asking that some measures might be taken looking toward our freedom. This document we all signed with pleasure."[13]

Finally, the Confederate authorities had had enough. At 9:00 A.M. on September 10, Gen. John Winder and an orderly entered the prison and announced that forty officers and a large number of privates were to be sent to Castle Pinckney in Charleston, South Carolina. A roll was read and the men were informed they were to be ready for the trip by one o'clock that afternoon. Colonel Corcoran was the first name announced for the transfer.

"God's will be done, I murmured within myself," admitted Corcoran. "I turned away to make ready a few little necessaries for my journey." Corcoran and the other prisoners bid one another sometimes tearful good-byes as they prepared for the move. "[D]uring the short time we had been together, " he continued, "attachments had been formed and friendships awakened . . . the scene reminded me more of the final parting of a family of loving brothers, than that of men who, a few weeks before, had, in the majority of instances, been perfect strangers to each other."[14]

When the hour arrived, the men, 154, were assembled in the street outside the prison and marched in a double line to the Petersburg Railroad accompanied by 50 guards from a Louisiana regiment commanded by Lt. W. B. Brockett.

"[S]elected chiefly from among those members of the New York, Massachusetts, and Michigan regiments who have evinced the most insolent and insubordinate disposition," reported the next day's Richmond *Examiner*, "[t]he invigorating sea-breezes, it is thought, and the genial climate of 'Dixie's Land,' will have the effect not only of improving the health, but also the temper of the captive Bull Runners."[15]

When the prisoners arrived in Charleston three days later, the conversion of Castle Pinckney into a POW facility was not quite finished. All of its guns had been moved out of its casemates but its arched openings were still in the process of being bricked up to form individual rooms. The prisoners were escorted from the train and marched through the streets to the Charleston City Jail, a large octagonal three-story stuccoed masonry building surmounted by a forty-foot-high brick tower. A walkout basement, fully exposed above ground to the rear, opened into a one-acre wall-enclosed prison yard. The 34 Union officers were placed in three rooms on the second floor of the main building while the 120 Union enlisted men were secured in twelve rooms on the uppermost floor. The facility was then temporarily placed under the command of Capt. Theodore G. Boag, Manigault's battalion, 6th South Carolina.

On September 18, renovation of the fort in the harbor was completed and the POWs were transferred.

"[T]wo abreast, we were filed into the fort," Corcoran related. "Here we were, as speedily as possible, organized into squads, or messes [and] each mess was assigned its particular quarters."[16]

The prisoners were housed nightly in the casemate dungeons, which were outfitted along three walls with three-tiered bunks, but were allowed to wander in and out of their rooms—restricted to the fort's interior parade grounds—during the daytime. Even under these conditions, the move to Charleston apparently had its desired affect. Although these men might have been discipline problems in Richmond, they remained content and well-behaved here. They willingly policed their own quarters, kept their casemates clean, got along well, and often bantered good-naturedly with their guards. Corcoran, especially, became a different prisoner and his changed attitude apparently influenced all the others.

"I must confess," wrote Corcoran,

> that about this time my heart was ready to sink beneath its load of sorrow. . . . I had expected that before this I would have been exchanged . . . yet, instead of such a pleasure, I was now being forced by my foes further and further from my home. . . . [I]n the midst of these gloomy reflections, I thought of what the martyr heroes of 1776 had done and suffered. I thought of Dartmore and the British prison-ships, in which thousands of the fathers of the Republic had endured ten times what I had endured. . . . Nevermore [I decided] should a complaint pass my lips.[17]

While these prisoners languished in their new quarters, further developments in this war were beginning to take hold elsewhere.

Back on the morning of July 6 in what would seem like a completely unrelated incident, the *Jefferson Davis,* a licensed privateer, overtook the *Enchantress,* a merchant schooner, off the southern coast of Delaware. Five seamen from the Confederate craft, under the command of Walter W. Smith, boarded the schooner, captured its crew, and confiscated $13,000 in cargo. Sixteen days later, while cruising under Confederate control, the *Enchantress* was, in turn, captured off Hatteras Inlet, North Carolina, by Union naval forces blockading the coast. Captain Smith and his crew were placed in irons and conveyed to Philadelphia for incarceration. The Union government refused to officially recognize these captured licensed privateersmen as prisoners of war. Instead, in an effort to eradicate the practice of privateering for the "unrecognized" government of the Confederacy, Union authorities brought charges of piracy and treason against them and threatened to have them hanged as pirates if they were found guilty.

On October 22, 1861, the privateersmen were placed on trial in what became known as the *Enchantress* Affair. A guilty verdict was returned against Captain Smith on October 25 and he was sentenced to death. Three of the other crew members were convicted three days later. As the remaining two awaited their fate, a crew of another privateer, the *Savannah*, captured by Union naval forces back on June 3 and being held in New York, was placed on trial there on the same charges.

"[T]his Government will deal out to the prisoners held by it the same treatment and the same fate as shall be experienced by those captured in the *Savannah*," Confederate president Jefferson Davis had originally threatened Union president Abraham Lincoln by letter three months before. "[T]here are other savage practices which have been resorted to by the Government of the United States which [must by repressed] by retaliation," he later informed the Congress of the Confederate States of America. Finally, in anticipation of the results of these "'sham' trials in the North, the Confederate congress passed an act officially authorizing their president to resort to that retaliation if needed.[18]

"You are hereby instructed to choose by lot from among the prisoners of war of highest rank," Acting Secretary of War Judah Benjamin, by order of Pres. Jefferson Davis, advised Brig. Gen. John H. Winder, once the verdicts against the *Enchantress* crew became known and the same fate appeared to be in store for the *Savannah* crew, "one who is to be confined in a cell appropriated to convicted felons . . . to be held for execution in the same manner as may be adopted by the enemy for the execution of the prisoner of war, [Walter W.] Smith recently condemned to death in Philadelphia. You will also select thirteen other prisoners of war, the highest in rank of those captured by our forces, to be confined in the cells reserved for prisoners accused of infamous crimes, and will treat them as such so long as the enemy shall continue so to treat the like number of prisoners of war captured by them at sea, and now held for trial in New York as pirates."[19]

The grim assignment was completed the following day. "The general in charge of this post, Brigadier-General Winder, with five or six other officers came into prison yesterday at 4 p.m.," relayed 1st Lt. John Whyte, 69th New York State Militia, in a letter dated November 11, 1861, "[and] called us officers to order and stated that he had an order from the War Department to ballot one out of the highest rank of the six colonels now prisoners of war in their possession and the one balloted and drawn to be placed in a cell in prison similar to that in which the condemned pirate Smith, at Philadelphia, is placed and to be disposed of according to his fate."[20]

"After the reading of this order," recalled prisoner Alfred Ely,

> he (General Winder) delivered to Colonel W. Raymond Lee of the 20th Massachusetts Regiment six slips of paper, upon which were written the names of the six Federal Colonels now held as prisoners of war by the Confederates, and requested him to . . . see that the names of the Colonels were upon the papers. Colonel Lee . . . declined, but General Winder insisted. When he read the name on each paper he folded and placed it in a tin tube nearly a foot long and only large enough to admit the hand. After shaking up the ballots, General Winder requested *me* to draw from the case a ballot and the Colonel whose name was drawn would be the one who should stand as hostage for the privateer Smith.[21]

Congressman Ely, too, refused to perform the requested task but finally relented upon the insistence of Winder and the reassurance of other POWs that it was okay. Reluctantly Ely drew the first ballot. It contained the name "Colonel Michael Corcoran."

"The Colonel was my messmate and intimate friend before he had been transferred from Richmond to South Carolina," Ely recalled sadly, "and great was my regret at finding that I had been the innocent cause of thus adding to his misfortune."[22]

"Mr. Ely and myself had . . . become very strongly attached to each other," Michael Corcoran later agreed. "I have not the slightest doubt that when he drew my name he felt far worse than I did . . . I had always been the object of their particular hatred and spleen, and of course I felt confident when the question of retaliation was settled, that I would be one of their first victims."[23]

The other hostages were picked in the same manner. "In choosing the thirteen [others] from the highest rank to be held to answer for a like number of prisoners of war captured by the enemy at sea," Brigadier General Winder advised the Confederate acting secretary of war, there being only ten field officers it was necessary to draw by lot three captains. The first names drawn were Capts. J[ames] B. Ricketts [U.S. Artillery], H[ugh W.] McQuaide [38th New York Volunteers] and G[eorge] W. Rockwood [15th Massachusetts Volunteers]. The list of thirteen will therefore stand—Colonels [W. Raymond] Lee [20th Massachusetts Volunteers], [Milton] Cogswell [42nd New York State Volunteers], [Orlando B.] Willcox [1st Michigan Volunteers], [William E.] Woodruff [2nd Kentucky Volunteers] and [Alfred M.] Wood [14th New York State Militia]; Lieutenant-Colonels [Samuel] Bowman [8th Pennsylvania Volunteers] and [George W.] Neff [2nd Kentucky Volunteers]; Majors [James D.] Potter [38th New York Volunteers], [Paul J.] Revere [20th Massachusetts Volunteers] and [Israel] Vogdes [U.S. Artillery].[24]

"When General Winder and his aids left the room," recalled prisoner William C. Harris, once all the names had been drawn and recorded by the Confederates, "we gathered in groups, eagerly discussing the principles of the policy, its bearing, causes, and effects."[25]

On November 12 Winder and his entourage returned to the prison and chose two other names to replace two originally chosen.

"In obedience to your instructions," Winder reported to Benjamin, "all the wounded officers have been exempted as hostages . . . I have therefore made selection by lot of Capts. H[enry] Bowman [15th Massachusetts Volunteers] and F[rancis] J. Keffer [Baker's California Regiment—actually the 71st Pennsylvania] to replace Captains Ricketts and McQuaide, wounded."[26]

"On the 14th of November we were called upon to bid them farewell," Harris continued. "As they passed from the room, we grasped each hand in silence; for, though the heart was steeled and the purpose steady, we could not, without emotions of heartfelt sympathy, see [them go]."[27]

The chosen hostages in Richmond were removed from Ligon's Military Prison and placed in cells of the Henrico County Jail, among the city's common criminals. Those who had been previously transferred to Charleston were informed of their fate and incarcerated among felons in the city jail there.

"[W]e received an intimation," recalled Corcoran, "that, as the pirates in the North were confined in prison cells as common felons, we would be served in the same manner . . . on the following Wednesday all the captives, myself included, were taken from our ocean-washed prison, and closely confined in the common jail in Charleston."[28]

Within only a few days Corcoran was placed in solitary confinement and shackled to the floor in one of seven "condemned cells" located in the upper tower of the Charleston city jail. "In the way of comfort," one prisoner wryly observed regarding these cells, "the Tombs [prison] in New York [is] a palace compared to them."[29]

"The Yankee prisoners in South Carolina are all safely lodged in jail," the *Charleston Mercury* proudly reported afterwards, "[and] they will abide the issue of the trials of our brave privateersmen in the North. Should one drop of Southern blood be shed by the Northern courts for defending the South on the seas, it will be paid with interest in Charleston."[30]

"They have threatened to retaliate upon their prisoners, life for life, the doom to which we consign ours" complained an indignant *New York Times,* "so that for every maritime thief we may adjudge to the gallows, they propose to measure out an equal length of hemp to the captives in their hands."[31]

"Self-protection," insisted the *Mercury,* "and the enforcement of the laws of nations and humanity, alike require, in this instance, full and ample retaliation."[32]

In the ensuing months a number of Northern and Southern newspapers continued to banter back and forth as both governments grappled with the issue and tried to save face. At the same time, the wives, families, and friends of the hostages of both sides bombarded Union and Confederate officials with letters and telegrams begging for mercy and British officials in Europe publicly announced their doubts about the legality of the Federal action.

"Privateering is a lawful mode of warfare," insisted Judge Charles P. Daly of New York, "and they wage war only against the Power with which the authority that commissioned them is at war."[33]

Judge Robert C. Grier of Philadelphia, a member of the tribunal that had originally tried Walter Smith, agreed, stating he could not understand why men taken on the sea should be hanged while those taken on land were held as prisoners or quite often exchanged.[34]

Title page of Col. Michael Corcoran's autobiography. AUTHOR'S COLLECTION

Finally, by January 1862, the Union began to backtrack in its get-tough policy once it realized it couldn't retain public support in treating privateersmen as pirates and criminals. Smith and his crew were quietly transferred from Philadelphia's Moyamensing Penitentiary to Fort Lafayette in New York harbor, where a number of political prisoners and POWs were being held, and Secretary Seward ordered Union major general John E. Wool to inquire whether Corcoran could be exchanged for Smith.

Immediately, Confederate major general Benjamin Huger, temporarily placed in charge of exchanges, noted that Wool's inquiry was a complete abandonment of the Union's previous declaration and advised his secretary of war.

Judah Benjamin instructed Huger to reply that no such proposition would be considered until there was "an unconditional abandonment of the pretext that [the privateersmen] are pirates and until they are released from the position of felons and placed in the same condition as other prisoners of war."[35]

At the same time, the jury in the *Savannah* case in New York was unable to reach a verdict. Union authorities then informed Confederate officials all the privateersmen had been moved to Fort Lafayette and that Smith's death sentence was countermanded. The Confederacy responded by declaring Corcoran would not be executed.

Meanwhile, throughout his imprisonment as a POW, Corcoran had remained immensely popular with the Irish and his subsequent selection as a hostage had aroused his fellow countrymen to a fevered pitch. They had protested the action loudly, regarding him as a martyr, and on February 5, 1862, they gathered at New York's Faneuil Hall to demand his immediate release.

"It is hoped that the rash indiscretion of persons pretending to be Colonel Corcoran's friends may not induce the rebels to prolong his imprisonment or refuse his exchange." declared Secretary of War Edwin M. Stanton.[36]

Perhaps such demonstrations did. Throughout the spring and into summer both governments continued to haggle over the exchanges. The crews of the *Savannah* and *Enchantress,* including Smith, were exchanged in May 1862, without any decision about Colonel Corcoran. Finally, resulting in a big reception in New York City, Corcoran and his attendant were released from captivity three months later, in August 1862.

"The fear of death was nothing," Corcoran later recalled somewhat cynically, "but to be brought down to the level of a skulking, cowardly pirate was a degradation that my soul revolted at."[37]

By the time this incident finally came to an end in the East, events had already developed in the West that would quickly draw the world's attention. Many of the same government officials involved in the Corcoran incident were about to find themselves deeply embroiled in additional controversies and retaliations much more devastating than this and with far worse results.

Chapter 3

The Palmyra Massacre

There seemingly was a long and extended history of violence taken against the POWs within the state of Missouri during this war. A border state torn apart by the conflict, sentiments there ran extremely high and involved four distinct groups of adversaries, each with their own intensely passionate feelings: militant secessionists, militant Unionists, moderates of Southern sympathies, and moderates of Union sympathies. Eventually the state provided more than 109,000 Union soldiers in 447 different military units and nearly 40,000 Confederate troops in more than 100 military units. At the same time, clashes of state militia units, the Regular Federal army units, the Confederate army units, and the various bands of guerrillas resulted in more than 1,160 battles and skirmishes across the state—a total that would only be exceeded in the states of Virginia and Tennessee.[1]

In a desperate effort to gain Union control over this region Brig. Gen. John M. Schofield, commanding the District of Missouri, issued General Orders No. 18 on May 29, 1862.

"The time is passed when insurrection and rebellion in Missouri can cloak itself under the guise of honorable War-Faro," declared Schofield in issuing the order. "The utmost vigilance and energy are enjoined upon all the troops of the State in hunting down and destroying these robbers and assassins. When caught in arms, engaged in their unlawful warfare, they will be shot down upon the spot."[2]

Simply taken, the soldiers in the field interpreted Orders No. 18 to mean "take no prisoners." Schofield later claimed that is not what he meant but by then it hardly mattered. The outright killing of POWs in Missouri had begun soon afterwards and the ruthless cold-blooded killings became almost an everyday occurrence by late that year.

"I make the rebels I shoot tell me all," boasted Maj. Haviland Tompkins, 13th Missouri State Militia Cavalry, in June 1862. Nor did Tompkins think it necessary that his prisoners he had shot wear a Confederate uniform. "I [once] arrested a minister and congregation," he continued. "I told them that they had to prove by acts that they loved our Government and we would [then] protect them and their property."[3]

Apparently the minister, a Reverend Wood of Phelps County, Missouri, was unable to satisfy that demand. Tompkins had members of the 5th Kansas Infantry shoot him as well as any of the congregation who protested. "A more attentive audience never listened to a man," bragged Tompkins. "I drew more tears than the minister."[4]

Tompkins was eventually responsible for the execution of a number of POWs. Finally, under public and political pressure Brigadier General Schofield ordered that Tompkins be arrested and the incidents investigated. Within a few short months Tompkins was exonerated and his command was restored. "I believe his country may expect much at his hands," boasted his commanding officer Col. John M. Glover, "and his country's enemies have much to fear."[5]

The Union received similar services from Lt. Alexander H. Lacy, 3rd Missouri Cavalry Volunteers, who was under the command of Capt. George S. Avery. Captain Avery continued to place groups of prisoners in Lacy's care, and they always soon afterwards "attempted to escape."

"[N]o body doubts that they fully deserved their fate," Lt. Col. Joseph Weydemeyer callously advised Colonel Glover regarding one such incident near Salem, Missouri, in August 1862. "The prisoners were delivered this forenoon to Captain Avery for transportation to Rolla, but soon after they had started[,] report came in that one of them, James Gallian, when about a mile distant from town had tried to run and was shot dead. I ordered the officer of the day to take a couple of men with pickaxes and spades to the spot to bury the man and ascertain the facts as far as possible. Very soon after that, Lieutenant Lacy came in and reported that about one mile and a half farther, the balance of the prisoners had found their end in the same way."[6]

Conditions for POWs in Missouri deteriorated quickly. By late 1862 the wholesale slaughter of prisoners became a common practice, causing many to be reluctant to surrender, and sometimes the pretense of an escape attempt was not even bothered with for those who did.[7]

"Our command captured two prisoners and they were turned over to me at this post as provost-marshal," complained Joseph B. Reavis of Waynesville, Missouri. "They surrendered to our command and were properly . . . placed under guard in the guard-house. Afterwards in the hours of the next night they were by the orders of Colonel [Albert] Sigel taken from the guard-house without my knowledge or consent and escorted to the woods where they were most inhumanely murdered."[8]

"I hope," Colonel Glover later cautioned Lieutenant Colonel Weydemeyer without actually telling him to stop, "you will counteract every impression that seems to indicate that we murder prisoners or indulge those who do. . . . [Those who surrender] only want assurances they are not to be shot when they come in to do so."[9]

Although many of these executions—such as the incident involving James Wilson and his men described in chapter one—were, admittedly, unofficially conducted by individuals in the field, several organized executions did "officially" take place during this same period. Probably the most infamous incident of this nature within the state of Missouri was the execution of ten Confederate prisoners of war in October 1862, in what became known as the "Palmyra Massacre."[10]

When Confederate colonel Joseph C. Porter's force of Missouri State Guards swept across northeast Missouri on a number of raids in the fall of 1862, one of his first orders was to take Marion County resident Andrew Allsman into custody.

Allsman was about sixty years old and had been a carpenter by trade before the war. A native of Kentucky, he had moved to Marion County, near Palmyra, Missouri, at the age of thirty-six. In time he became well known throughout the county and by 1860 he was generally known to be an ardent Union man. When war broke out he quickly enlisted and served briefly in the 3rd Missouri State Militia (Union) Cavalry but because of his age he was sent home to serve as a home guardsman. That too failed to work out for Allsman, however, because the prevalent sympathies in the Palmyra area were for the South. Allsman remained unpopular after his return, and before long, he was serving as a Union informant, providing information to the Federal authorities as to the loyalty or disloyalty of particular residents and leading Union troops to the homes of Southern sympathizers.

"So efficiently and successfully did he act in these various capacities," reported the Palmyra *Courier*, "that he won the bitter hatred of all the rebels in this city and vicinity."[11]

Porter's order for Allsman's arrest fell on Capt. J. W. Shuttuck, himself a recent escapee from Gratiot Street Prison in St. Louis where he had been held as a political prisoner based on information provided by Allsman.

"Allsman," declared Griffin Frost, a member of Co. A, Missouri State (Confederate) Guards at the time, "was about the meanest man in Marion county."[12]

Confederate troops proceeded to round up a number of prisoners in the area and several, including Allsman, were arrested at their homes and taken away. Just west of the city the prisoners were halted in a field of the Berkley Summer's farm where all but Allsman and three others were paroled and sent on their way. Exactly what happened next is uncertain. Upon learning of the Confederate raid on Palmyra, Union forces led by Col. John McNeil, 2nd Missouri Militia Cavalry, pursued Porter's troops. McNeil's soldiers caught up with the Confederates a few days later, and a skirmish ensued at Whaley's Mill, in the northeast corner of Shelby County, where both sides lost three men and several captured. Two of the Confederates captured by Union troops were charged with being "oath breakers," taken to a nearby field the following day, and shot. Sometime afterward it is believed fleeing Confederate troops halted at nearby Troublesome Creek where they executed Andrew Allsman, either out of retaliation or to prevent being slowed in their escape—or both.[13]

Although Allsman's body was never found, rumors persisted throughout Marion County that he had been killed. Confederate authorities, on the other hand, maintained they had no idea what happened to him—they had simply released him to facilitate their flight.

"[T]his is to notify you," proclaimed a public notice issued October 8, 1862, to the citizens of Marion County by Provost-Marshal William R. Strachan under orders of Col. John McNeil, "that unless said Andrew Allsman is returned to his family within ten days from this date, ten men [of the Confederate forces] who are now in custody will be shot."[14]

No one doubted the voracity of McNeil's proclamation. His ruthless, cold-blooded reputation was already well established in the vicinity. Nearly

Col. John McNeil, who gained a
ruthless reputation in northeast
Missouri for authorizing so many
mass executions of Confederate
POWs. LIBRARY OF CONGRESS

everyone knew that he was responsible for a number of prisoner deaths throughout Missouri, including the previously well publicized execution of seventeen POWs—that of Col. Frisby H. McCullough, 2nd Division, Missouri State Guard, and sixteen privates—whom his troops had captured during a battle at Kirksville the previous August—and another ten POWs at Macon, Missouri, the following September.[15]

John McNeil was a Canadian, born in Nova Scotia. He was a hatter before the war, having learned his trade in Boston before moving to St. Louis to establish his business. While in that city he later started an insurance company, entered politics, and was eventually elected to the Missouri State Legislature. With the outbreak of war, he obtained a colonel's commission, first in the 3rd Missouri U.S. Reserve Corps in May 1861, and then in the 2nd Missouri Militia Cavalry at the expiration of the 3rd's three-month term of service. Within months of its formation McNeil's command was regarded as a well-trained, elite cavalry that quickly gained a reputation for barbarity. McNeil, himself, was considered a hard-core unrelenting disciplinarian.[16]

At the time of his October 8 ultimatum there were about forty POWs confined in the county jails at Palmyra and Hannibal, Missouri. On Octo-

ber 17, McNeil ordered the provost marshal to list ten of those men to execute. Strachan selected five from each prison; he then ordered authorities
at Hannibal to have the five selected from there transported to Palmyra.
Walking down to the Palmyra Marion County Jail, on the corner of
Lafayette and Dickerson streets across from the courthouse, he personally
notified the five there of their fate. Soon afterward, Rev. James S. Green
was alerted and proceeded to the jail to offer spiritual consolation to the
condemned.

"I found them excited and alarmed," advised Reverend Green, "but
ready, like brave, courageous men, to meet their fate with fortitude."[17]

Green spoke to the men at great length about their fate and before he
left suggested they forgive McNeil and Strachan.

"They are ruthless murderers who are taking the lives of ten innocent
men," declared Willis Baker, one of the POWs chosen to be executed. "I
will see them in hell before I'll forgive 'em!"[18]

The ten who were selected were Capt. Thomas A. Sidenor, a young
man in his early twenties from Monroe County who had shoulder-length
dark hair and was engaged to be married; Eleazer Lake of Scotland County,
who was married and had a number of children; Thomas Humston from
Lewis County and the youngest of all ten at nineteen; Morgan Bixler, also
of Lewis County, who upon learning of his fate sat down and wrote his
wife and two sons a touching letter that was later published in the local
newspaper; William T. Humphrey, of Lewis County, married with six children; Willis T. Baker, fourth of the group from Lewis County, and the oldest at sixty; John Y. McPheeters of Marion County; and Herbert Hudson,
John M. Wade, and Francis Marion Lair, all from Ralls County. All of
these men had, at one time or another, served under Porter except for
Baker, a Southern sympathizer jailed after being accused of killing his pro-
Union neighbor. None of these men had been tried for anything. Most
were merely prisoners of war captured during a skirmish. A number of
those had since been accused of violating previous oaths "not to take up
arms against the Federal government," but even in those cases no formal
charges, trials, proceedings, or courts-martial had taken place. And even
Baker had denied the charges brought against him and was still awaiting a
trial. Not one of these men had been convicted of anything.

"[O]n the night before the execution," recalled one Marion County
resident,

The Marion County Jail building in Palmyra, Missouri, as it appears today.
LONNIE R. SPEER

one of the most prominent citizens of Palmyra went to [General] McNeil and asked him if he could not or would not stop the execution—that he was about to take the lives of ten innocent men for one, who was of no earthly account [anyway]. . . . A petition was also gotten up for the purpose of having the execution postponed ten days, thinking that by seeing General Schofield, who was then in command of the Department of the Missouri, he might be prevailed upon to stay the execution altogether . . . but all [was] to no purpose.[19]

Early Saturday morning, October 18, the day of the scheduled execution, Mrs. Mary Humphrey frantically rushed over to the provost marshal's office to beg for her husband's life. Arriving in Palmyra the afternoon before to visit her jailed husband, she was completely unaware of his pending fate. It was after she completed her visit and left the jail that Strachan arrived to

The doorway from which guards escorted the condemned Confederates to waiting wagons that would transport them to the execution site. LONNIE R. SPEER

notify the condemned prisoners. Upon learning of the sentence, Mrs. Humphrey was devastated. She, along with two of her six children, a baby and a nine-year-old daughter, pleaded with Strachan to reconsider. He told her it was out of his hands. She then went to McNeil's headquarters and pleaded with him. McNeil denied her request and sent her away. Outside Mary told her daughter to go in and beg for her father's life or they would never see him again. The little girl did and within a short time Colonel Mc-Neil appeared at his office doorway, handed Mrs. Humphrey a note, and told her to take it to the provost marshal. She and the children returned to Strachan's office and after reading the note, which advised him to find some reason to spare Humphrey and replace him with a prisoner with no family, the provost marshal chose Hiram Smith as a suitable replacement.

Smith was a young man of twenty-two from Knox county. Two of his brothers had married daughters of Willis Baker so the two felt some kinship toward one another. When Strachan entered the jail to inform Smith of his fate, he found him with Baker taking messages that were to be conveyed to various members of the family. Strachan walked up and informed Smith he had also been selected to be executed at 1:00 P.M.

Smith glared at Strachan for a moment before walking away, apparently accepting the decision as inevitable and realizing it was fruitless to argue. Since he could not write, Smith went to another prisoner and asked to dictate a letter to his sister.

A little after noon three government flatbed freight wagons containing rough-board coffins drove up to the jail. Three coffins had been loaded onto two of the wagons while the third wagon contained four. The ten condemned men were conducted from the prison and seated in the back of the wagons, one upon each coffin. The procession, flanked and followed by Federal soldiers and gathering civilians, slowly proceeded down the street and out toward the fairgrounds on the east end of town. On the way it passed the residence of Joseph McPheeters, uncle of John, one of the condemned.

"[T]he atmosphere was made to resound with the heart rending shrieks of relatives gathered there," recalled one Palmyra resident.[20]

A half-mile east of town the wagons halted in the Marion County Fairgrounds within the circular amphitheater ring. The ten coffins were dragged from the wagons to the center of the ring and placed in a row six to eight feet apart, forming a line north and south, about fifteen paces east

William R. Strachan's provost marshal headquarters in Palmyra, Missouri, as it appears today. LONNIE R. SPEER

of the central pagoda or music stand. Each coffin was positioned upon the ground, with its foot west and head east. Thirty soldiers of the 2nd Missouri State Militia, with an additional line of reserves behind them, formed up in tight formation facing the row of coffins from a distance of about thirteen paces. As the executioners watched, the doomed men knelt upon the grass in front of their coffins as Rev. R. M. Rhodes said a prayer.

"At the conclusion of this," reported the Palmyra *Courier,* "each prisoner took his seat upon the foot of his coffin, facing the muskets. . . . They were nearly all firm and undaunted . . . two or three only showing signs of trepidation."[21]

Reverend Rhodes and Provost Marshal Strachan passed down the line of coffins shaking hands with the prisoners. All mechanically offered their hands as the two passed except Willis Baker, who refused to shake Strachan's. Blindfolds were offered the men but only the first two, Humston and Bixler, accepted. When they saw the others refuse, they both tossed theirs to the ground.

About a hundred spectators stood quietly off in the distance. The prisoners remained seated on their coffins. Neither their hands nor their feet were tied in any manner. There was nothing that forced them to stay in position. Some fidgeted, some simply stared at their executioners, and some simply looked away, down at the ground in front of them.

"Aim here," Sidenor said as he broke the silence and placed his hand up to the left side of his chest.[22]

"Make ready!" yelled the commanding officer, Maj. Isham B. Dodson. "Aim!" came his second order. Then, after a moment of silence, he gave the final command: "Fire!"[23]

For whatever reason, the line of executioners failed to discharge their weapons simultaneously. A volley rattled off sporadically down the line as two of the POWs flopped over backward upon their coffins and died instantly. At the same time Sidenor lurched from his seat and fell dead on the ground in front of his coffin, face up, eyes wide-open with his head and neck arched backward looking eerily at the gunmen. Six of the others were wounded to various degrees and lay writhing on the ground, wallowing in their own blood; Morgan Bixler hadn't been hit at all. He immediately jumped up as if he had won some kind of macabre lottery, only to slip in a nearby puddle of pooling blood and fall down.[24]

"Second line forward!" screamed Major Dodson as the reserves, revolvers drawn, raced forward to finish the POWs off. Small groups stood over each man and fired continuously until the yelling, moving, jerking, or quivering stopped. Bixler was dispatched almost immediately while sixty-year-old Willis Baker was the last to die, requiring seven bullets to finally kill him.[25]

The crowd of onlookers, stunned and dazed by the grotesque exhibition, quietly wandered away. The Federal troops stood around for some time looking at the carnage without a word. Finally, the order was given to place the bodies into the coffins and to load them onto the wagons for the trip back to town.

Once back in Palmyra, the coffins were unloaded and left in front of the county courthouse. By that evening all but three had been claimed and

An illustration by Palmyra resident James B. Settles depicting the October 18, 1862 execution. AUTHOR'S COLLECTION

removed by family and friends for burial. The remaining coffins were buried by Federal troops in the town cemetery.[26]

The Palmyra *Courier* ran a full account of the event the following day. Although the morbid details were omitted, they were already the talk of the community and quickly spread throughout the county. Soon, the event was being referred to as a "massacre."

The *Courier* account was reprinted in the November 3 issue of the *Memphis Daily Appeal* and, subsequently, appeared in additional newspapers throughout the South. With continued circulation of the report, shock and indignation spread across the Confederacy and eventually overseas.

"The story of this terrible act of bloodshed," declared an editorial in the *London Star,* "will form probably the most painful episode upon which the mind of an American can hereafter dwell when reviewing the incidents of this war."[27]

"It seems incredible," wrote a correspondent from Paris, "that Americans can to-day forget their boasts about the land which was to serve as a beacon-light to humanity."[28]

During this time, the incident also came to the attention of Confederate president Jefferson Davis.

"[A]scertain if the facts are as stated," Davis demanded of Lt. Gen. Theophilus H. Holmes, commander of Confederate troops in the Trans-Mississippi Department. "If they be so, you will demand the immediate surrender of General McNeil to the Confederate authorities, and if this demand is not complied with, you will inform said commanding officer that you are ordered to execute the first ten United States officers who may be captured and fall into your hands."[29]

Holmes passed the directive on to Maj. Gen. Samuel R. Curtis, commander of Union forces, Department of the Missouri.

"You have no military power in Missouri," Curtis informed Holmes in a reply that defended McNeil, "much less a civil organization which would induce any man to call himself a 'Confederate citizen.' There is but one class of 'citizens of Missouri[']; they are Federal citizens, not Confederate. . . . The rights of such citizens cannot be adjudicated by appeal through the military authorities of the so-called Confederate States. I have no disposition to overlook the conduct of any officer in my command or shift any responsibility which it may attach to me, but while the State of Missouri can guard her own citizens through the regularly constituted authorities I cannot even by implication justify any interference by you."[30]

More simply put, Curtis advised Holmes and President Davis to mind their own business, indicating that if Missouri or Federal authorities decided to execute their citizens it was no one else's concern. On November 29, 1862, McNeil was promoted to brigadier general and continued in command of the District of Northern Missouri.[31]

Such belligerent attitudes did nothing more than fuel another round of death threats back and forth throughout the following months. With the controversy surrounding Corcoran still unresolved in the East at that time and contentions over the Palmyra incident increasing in the West, no one should be surprised that the war of retaliation would greatly intensify in the coming month.

Chapter 4

"The Designs of the Mob"

GAINESVILLE

By the fall of 1862 it was just as dangerous for Union sympathizers to live in northeast Texas as it was for Confederate sympathizers to live in northeast Missouri. The Butterfield Overland Mail Route, established in 1858, extended from St. Louis through Fort Smith, Arkansas, and down into northern and west central Texas before continuing west on into California. The new stagecoach route brought a gradual migration of new residents into the region from the East, North, and Midwest. Within two years the overwhelming majority of the north Texas population was from the states of Missouri, Kansas, Arkansas, Illinois, Indiana, Tennessee, and Kentucky, drastically changing the character of this part of the state. By 1860, less than 10 percent of the north Texas population owned slaves, a fact uncharacteristic of the deep South.[1]

Although a majority of the state's population eventually voted to secede from the Union, officially withdrawing on March 2, 1861, eleven northern counties, centered around Cooke and Grayson Counties, voted overwhelmingly against it. Shortly after secession had passed, E. Junius Foster, editor of the Sherman *Patriot* in Grayson County, suggested that the eleven northern counties separate from Texas to form a new free state. He began a petition drive soon afterwards to initiate his proposal and three of the region's most ardent and outspoken Unionists, Henry Chiles, Alexander D. Scott, and Leander W. P. "Jacob" Lock, joined in the effort. This eleven-county area, which included Cooke, Grayson, Montague, Fannin, Jack,

Wise, Denton, Collin, Parker, Tarrant, and Dallas, was bounded on the east and west by great expanses of dense woodland known as the Eastern and Western Cross Timbers, on the south by the Grand Prairie, and on the north by the Red River. The possibility of the district separating from the rest of the state aroused great passion on both sides and sparked a heated controversy throughout the region for several months. Adding fuel to the fire, the Confederate conscription act was passed a year later on April 16, 1862, requiring all able-bodied white males between the ages of eighteen and thirty-five to join the military. The law was openly defied in some areas but it became most evident in this region as widespread protests erupted. By the following May, Gen. Paul O. Hébert, commander of the Military Department of Texas, declared martial law and appointed provost marshals to enforce the conscription law.[2]

In Grayson County thirty prominent, outspoken citizens from the various surrounding counties gathered in the private home of Clement C. Woods to discuss their opposition to the conscription law and to propose some formal plan of action against it. Their opposition mainly focused on the exemptions that large slaveholders had from the draft. According to the conscription law, substitutes were allowed for draftees who could afford it and all slaveholders or plantation overseers working twenty or more slaves were exempt from military service all together. Samuel McNutt, a forty-nine-year-old carpenter originally from New York who drew up a petition protesting the exemptions, fully intended to take it to Richmond and submit it to the Confederate Congress in an effort to get the Conscription Act nullified. In addition to Woods and McNutt, some of the others in attendance included Henry Chiles and his brother Ephraim, both of whom moved to the area from Missouri in 1860, A. D. Scott, Jacob Lock, Henry S. Field, M. D. Harper, William W. Morris, Jackson H. Mounts, Obediah B. Atkinson, Rev. Hydeman P. Garrison, and Newton J. Chance. Everyone at the meeting was thought to be a passionate Unionist and everyone present did sign the petition; however, Newton Chance privately regarded the petition as a treasonous document. He requested a copy of the petition for himself before it was turned over to Atkinson, an early Cooke County pioneer and one of the leading pro-Union men in the group, who was in charge of getting the document to the Confederate capital.[3]

Twenty-nine-year-old Newt Chance seemed to be an impulsive fellow. He was originally an Illinois blacksmith who moved to Kansas for a short time before recently settling in Denton County, Texas, with his wife and two children. He had joined a Tarrant County volunteer regiment at the outbreak of the war, resigned, helped organize a company for the 14th Texas Cavalry, was discharged, joined the 9th Texas Cavalry, was discharged again, and then served in an intelligence company before being discharged once more—all of this accomplished before August 1862. Vehement in all that he did, it was apparently doubted by no one at the clandestine meeting that he had become a pro-Union man, and he was unquestionably provided a copy of the petition.[4]

A few days later Newt Chance took his personal copy of the petition to Lt. Col. James G. Bourland, provost marshal of Cooke County, who was headquartered in the county seat of Gainesville, and informed him of the Grayson County meeting.

Bourland, sixty years old, was a slave owner and ardent secessionist. Originally from South Carolina, he had moved to the Red River valley in 1837 and established a large cotton plantation on the rich river bottomland. Upon hearing the details of the meeting and reviewing the petition, Lieutenant Colonel Bourland led troops over to McNutt's homestead and ran him out of the county under the threat of death.

Lieutenant Colonel Bourland had hoped McNutt's exile would destroy all organized resistance to the conscription act in the county. It only served, however, to intensify an increasingly subversive opposition. The remaining twenty-eight members of the "Grayson Thirty" began to organize and recruit a secret society, complete with a password, a secret sign or hand signal, and a grip or secret handshake. Within a short time, Confederate authorities in the region began to hear rumors of the existence of a Unionist organization that went under a variety of names—the Union League, the Peace Party, the Clan, and the Order—which possibly had a membership of nearly 1,700 sympathizers.

In September 1862, the conscription law was revised to include all white males between the ages of seventeen and fifty, intensifying the region's opposition that was now being organized quietly. Later that same month Pvt. Jonas B. McCurley, a Confederate mail carrier of the Denton County Rangers, was staying at the Foreman's Hotel in Gainesville. While sitting in the lobby that evening he was approached by a man later determined to be Unionist farmer Ephraim Chiles. Chiles was intoxicated and struck up a conversation with McCurley, telling him about an organization known as the "Order" in an attempt to recruit him, hinting of an impending attack on the Confederate arsenals in Gainesville and Sherman.

"This man told the mail-carrier enough about this organization to excite his curiosity and his suspicion," recalled Thomas Barrett, a Cooke County physician and Disciples of Christ minister, "so he asked a number of questions about it; the intoxicated man told him to go to a certain man and that man would initiate him and tell him all about it. The mail-carrier said nothing about what he had heard, but started south with the mail next morning."[5]

McCurley thought about many of the details of Childs's boasting during his day's ride toward Denton County. Once he arrived he reported the conversation to a Confederate officer who encouraged him to report the incident and, in fact, passed it on to Provost Marshal Bourland in Gainesville.

Within a few days McCurley returned to provide the details firsthand to Bourland.

"When this mail-carrier came back to Gainesville," Barrett continued, "the military questioned him and after learning all they could from him, he was sent to be initiated."[6]

Lieutenant Colonel Bourland had relayed McCurley's information to his superior, Brig. Gen. William R. Hudson, and other military authorities in the area, and they all agreed it would be a great advantage if McCurley could infiltrate the organization and gather more information on the group's members and their intentions.

Dr. Henry Chiles, Ephraim's brother, was the contact man McCurley had been told about at the hotel. Two weeks after his military debriefing McCurley was provided a horse by Bourland and sent out to Dr. Chiles's homestead in a feigned search for stray livestock. During a brief conversation, McCurley mentioned having met the doctor's brother and expressed interest in joining the Order. After further talk, Henry Chiles escorted McCurley into the house where he was sworn to secrecy and given an oath in the "first degree" of initiation similar to that experienced by Masons or Odd Fellows. He learned that the organization's password was "Arizona" and their grip was an altered handshake similar to those used in the Masonic lodges. With his first initiation McCurley also learned the organization planned a general uprising when enough members had joined, that certain members regularly exchanged letters with a Unionist organization in Kansas, and that perhaps once Federal invading forces reached the capital at Austin, James H. Lane, the Kansas senator and abolitionist, might be installed as the Texas governor, resulting in Union control being restored and the killing of all Secessionists. When McCurley asked for the names of other members so that he might know them on sight, he was told that members only identified one another by signs and communicated in code and no more information would be revealed unless he wished to take the "second degree" of initiation. Upon learning the details of what that might consist of, McCurley declined the offer and left.[7]

Upon hearing the new details, Colonel Bourland wanted the information that would come with the second-degree initiation and requested that McCurley return. He refused so Newt Chance was approached and arrangements were made for him to communicate with Childs about joining the Order.

Within a few days Newt Chance and his brother Joseph had been initiated in the first and second degrees of the Union League and reported back to Colonel Bourland.

"[H]e must take an oath," they reported about the second-degree initiation, "to do all he could for the north and all he could against the south [and] he was to endeavor to reinstate the constitution and union, and kill any member who should betray them."[8]

With the second-degree initiation came the secrets of identifying other members using the sign, the grip, and the password of the organization.

"[A]fter taking it they were told when they met up with a man," one witness revealed,

> to pass the fingers of the right hand slowly over the right ear; the answer . . . was for the man to pass the finger of the left hand slowly over the left ear. . . . [T]o be sure he understood and answered the sign, he was to be asked where he got his horse or any article about him. If he said in 'Arizona,' he . . . could be approached. The grip to distinguish [a member] in a crowd or in the dark consisted of the common shake of the hand with the end of the forefinger pressing tolerably hard on the inside of the wrist.[9]

Lieutenant Colonel Bourland and Brigadier General Hudson and a number of others believed the Order represented a great threat and an immediate danger to the entire region.

"Their plans were to rise in the night, take all the ammunition at Sherman and Gainesville and throw the country," worried Barrett, "and no man's person or property was to be respected unless he had their sign, password and grip."[10]

Once the Chance brothers had been interviewed and the reports were filed, Bourland, Hudson, and Col. Daniel Montague, commander of the local Cooke County Militia, began making arrangements to mobilize their troops. All Cooke County units were ordered to report to Gainesville at once while one company was ordered from Wise, Denton, and Grayson counties and one was asked for and sent from Fort Washita, in nearby Indian Territory. While awaiting the arrival of these out-of-town troops, squads of local militia and civil authorities fanned out across the county on the night of September 30 and surrounded many homes in the darkness to keep suspected members of the Order under surveillance. At dawn, October 1, 1862, with the arrival of additional troops, the militia and civil authorities swept in on the homes and began making arrests.

At the Obediah Atkinson home, he and his friend John Davidson, whose families shared the house, placed mattresses over their backs and fled out the back door under a hail of gunfire. Hiram Kilborn, a Baptist lay minister, tried to flee from his home too, but was shot and killed. By midday nearly seventy men had been arrested and incarcerated in a vacant Gainesville store, on the ground floor of the Downer Building on the public square. Armed guards were posted all around the building. Some of those arrested included leaders Dr. Henry Chiles, Ephraim Chiles, Clem Woods, Henry Field, M. D. Harper, Leander Lock, William Morris, Thomas B. Floyd, James T. Foster, and many others. Arrests were made of suspected members throughout the eleven northern counties.

"The arresting continued for about thirteen days and nights," admitted Gainesville resident Thomas Barrett. "How many were arrested I have no means of knowing, having kept no account at the time, but I suppose there was not less than one hundred and fifty, and perhaps more."[11]

A "citizens' court" convened on the afternoon of October 1 on the second floor of the Rufus F. Scott store, on the Gainesville square. Colonel

Bourland appointed a jury and placed his old friend and colleague Col. William C. Young, 11th Texas Cavalry, home because of ill health, chairman. Once the jury was chosen, they selected court officers. Longtime resident Ralph G. Piper was appointed chief justice, Colonel Young was appointed prosecutor, Col. Daniel Montague, jury foreman, Piper and James M. Peery, court clerks, and William W. Bourland, son of Colonel Bourland, constable. All of these men, it should be noted, were slave owners. In fact, Colonel Bourland and Colonel Young, together, owned nearly 25 percent of the total number of slaves in Cooke County while at the same time, seven of the twelve jurors were also slave owners.

"Soon after I arrived on the square I heard hanging spoken of," resident Tom Barrett, a slave owner and one of those chosen for the jury, admitted, "[and] I found the tree had [already] been selected—that same old historic elm, with its long and bending limbs," at the end of California Street.[12]

"When I got there everything was in confusion," recalled William C. West, another eyewitness. "I found several of my neighbors there under guard . . . I knew they was all Union men and voted the Union ticket and also put their names to [a] petition asking the Confederate Congress to remove that exemption law."[13]

Once the court officers and jury had been seated, policy and procedure were argued. The accused were all farmers who did not own slaves and most had been eligible for Confederate military service but had refused or failed to join. The Confederate, slave-holding officers in charge of the court and the majority of the jury, who were also slave-holders, insisted that conviction should rest on a majority vote. Barrett and a few others argued that conviction should be based on a unanimous or at least a two-thirds vote. The majority in the room rejected the idea and passed the majority rule.

As the organizers continued their struggle to give the assemblage some appearance of an authentic court of justice, four men, Piper, Aaron Hill, Cincinnatus Potter, and Irish immigrant James E. Sheegog, were appointed to serve as a committee of inquiry to question witnesses and make a record of their testimony, and Ralph Piper was further assigned to swear in defendants and witnesses. That evening Piper swore in the twelve jurors and the court adjourned until the next day. That night a double line of sentinels were placed around Gainesville at a distance of a half mile in fear that the town might be attacked by the Union League to rescue their members. "Squads of men were sent to different parts of the county," Barrett recalled, "to ascertain what was going on, for an attack was expected."[14]

No attack came, however, so the court reconvened on the morning of October 2. The first defendant led into the room was Dr. Henry Chiles. Accused of treason and conspiracy, he refused legal counsel, pleaded not guilty, and conducted his own defense. Newton and Joseph Chance testified against him as did Jonas McCurley and several others.

"The excitement had increased," related Barrett. "It was terrible with the crowd outside, and no less so in the jury-room. . . . Those opposed to extreme punishment found it necessary to be extremely cautious if they made a remark in favor of mercy."[15]

The jury quickly convicted Chiles by a majority vote and sentenced him to be hanged on October 4. His brother Ephraim was led into the courtroom next. After brief testimony by the same witnesses, Ephraim, too, was found guilty and sentenced to be hanged in two days. They were both turned over to the military as two additional leaders of the Union League, Henry Field, a forty-five-year-old shoemaker who was married and had three children, and M. D. Harper, a thirty-one-year-old married carpenter also having three children, were led into the court one at a time that day, each charged with "conspiracy and insurrection" or "disloyalty and treason." Field had little to say in his defense while Harper became angry at the jury's verdict condemning him to be hanged and yelled defiantly at them as he was led out of the room.[16]

Although the official date of all four executions had been set for October 4, a few hours after the last trial a wagon pulled up to the Downer Building and Henry Chiles was led out. Escorted to the wagon by the military, Chiles was directed to the bed and surrounded by guards. The wagon was driven by Bob Scott, a slave owned by Rufus Scott, owner of the store where the trials had taken place. Surrounded by a large number of armed men, citizens, and the military, the wagon was driven slowly down California Street to the edge of town, where it was brought to a halt at a large elm along the bank of Pecan Creek. There Lt. Alexander Boutwell, former Cooke County sheriff, read the orders of execution while ropes were thrown over the elm's enormous arching branches and a noose was arranged around Dr. Chiles's neck as he stood on the wagon bed. Pale and trembling, he undoubtedly heard Boutwell order Bob Scott to drive the wagon out from beneath the tree. The wagon pulled out and, slowly, Chiles strangled as he was left dangling above the ground.[17]

After about an hour the military returned to the makeshift jail with Scott and escorted Ephraim Chiles out. Arriving at Pecan Creek, they took

Henry's body down in front of Ephraim and then hanged him using the same procedure.[18]

The following day Jacob Lock and William Morris were tried and condemned. None of these defendants had an opportunity to obtain a defense attorney, to cross-examine any of the witnesses against them, or to call witnesses on their behalf. But it probably made no difference anyway. They were quickly found guilty by a majority vote of the jury and sentenced to be hanged.

The next morning court reconvened concentrating on the Union League's rank and file members. Many testified that they knew nothing about the organization beyond the "first degree" while others maintained the group was known to them only as the "Peace Party," offering protection through neutrality.

"I am fully and completely satisfied," confided Barrett, "that many of those who were duped, imposed on, and got into this organization, never would have gone into this clan if they had known the dark and bloody intentions of the leaders. But these men were sworn to obey their leaders if the uprising had taken place . . . and the dark designs would have been carried out."[19]

On October 4, while the court was hearing testimony and deciding the fate of others, Lieutenant Boutwell and his soldiers took Henry Field and M. D. Harper out to Pecan Creek and hanged them. Leander Lock was taken out on October 7 and William Morris met his fate on October 8.

During those same days a number of men were acquitted but on Friday, October 10, Dr. James T. Foster and Thomas B. Floyd, a friend of William Morris, broke away from their guards as they were being led from the courtroom back to the Downer building. Both men were shot and killed in their attempt to escape. That same afternoon Edward D. Hampton was convicted and sentenced to be hanged that afternoon. When another acquaintance of Barrett was convicted on the slimmest of evidence soon afterwards, he and another juror protested and threatened to quit the jury. Other members convinced them to stay—if for no other reason than to help prevent *everyone* from being convicted and hanged. The two decided to remain when changes were agreed upon.

"I had influenced the jury to adopt the two-thirds rule," proclaimed Barrett, "which stopped the hanging for a while . . . [w]e had some hot contentions in the jury-room but we either set the men at liberty or decided to send them to the headquarters of the military authorities."[20]

Meanwhile, the crowd outside became more and more agitated as the day wore on. Finally a large mob stormed the Downer building and demanded that the guards open the door. They refused and drew their weapons. The crowd left but they had become so excited that they proceeded directly to the town jail where they seized the only occupant, a man accused of being a horse thief and deserter from the Confederate army, and lynched him.[21]

The next day, Saturday, October 11, the jury continued to review cases and hear testimony, operating under the two-thirds rule. No one was sentenced to be hanged. In fact, a few were set free. The ever-present mob standing by outside on the town square, however, didn't like the results and then learned of the so-called "two-thirds rule."

"Some person betrayed us and told the crowd outside of our decision," complained one juror, "and a mob rose and sent two men into the juryroom with word that if we did not give up twenty more to be hung, they would kill every man in the prison. . . . [O]ne of these men called for a list of the names of the prisoners. Our clerk handed it to him, and he went over it; took such men as he chose and wrote their names down, then handed the list back to the clerk, and called over the names he had and our clerk marked them out. He then counted his names and he had fourteen. He said as he rose from his seat: 'I reckon this will satisfy them.'"[23]

These men proceeded over to the makeshift prison, presented the list to the guards, and informed the fourteen named men they were to be hanged on the following day, Sunday. They were then moved into a separate room of the building to be isolated from the other prisoners.

Consequently, the jurors of the citizens' court decided to adjourn for a week. Some, including Barrett, hoped the rage throughout the county would subside by then.

After church on Sunday afternoon, October 12, Tom Barrett wandered over to the Foreman Hotel on the northeast side of the square and took a seat on the porch.

"I had not been there long," he recalled, "till I saw the death wagon coming with two of the prisoners. I saw men with guns on each side of the wagon guarding, to prevent escape, and see that the hanging was done, and this was continued till late in the evening before the last one was hung."[23]

Throughout the day the hangings continued two at a time, sometimes with the next two victims having to watch the previous two meet their fate.

Even more surprising to Barrett, the "men with guns" guarding the prisoners were soldiers!

"I saw that the military authorities had detailed men to carry out the designs of the mob," he continued. "Can it be possible that the military authorities knew that these men were taken from the jury and are being hung, contrary to [the jury's] decision, or are they in with the mob?"[24]

Barrett claimed he could never be sure but it was very apparent to everyone else that the Confederate authorities were just as deeply involved with these hangings as they had been with those previously sanctioned by the citizens' court. Since the hanging of all fourteen victims could not be completed that Sunday, the procession continued throughout the following Monday.

"They would take 4 or 5 on the wagon at a time," recalled James Lemuel Clark, who was an eighteen-year-old soldier in the state militia, serving out of town, when his father, Nathaniel Miles Clark, became one of the hanging victims, "[and] haul them down on a little creek in the east part of town and murder them, [then haul them back] and throw their bodies in an old house that was up near the square."[25]

A slave named Frank Foreman, owned by W. W. Foreman, the hotel owner, was detailed to build coffins for the dead men.

"He says they made him and another fellow tear down an old house that was in the north part of town to get lumber to make the boxes," advised Clark.[26]

Bodies claimed by family members were turned over to them for private burial, otherwise they were taken back and buried in the bank along the creek. In some cases, bodies claimed by their families were delivered and buried by the men who hanged them.

"[T]o give some idea as to how things was carried [out]," insisted Clark, "old man W[illiam]. W. Wernell was hung in Gainesville and brought to his wife and children. The men that brung him went and buried him, and put his head north. They said he wanted to go north [so] they would put his head north. His grave is here to show the facts."[27]

Although nearly eighty men remained confined in the town's makeshift prison, the citizen's court made no plans to reconvene before Saturday, October 18.

"During this week of adjournment," declared Barrett, "I went to town every day, and the excitement was moderating, and everything bidding fair

The February 20, 1864, Frank Leslie's Illustrated Weekly Newspaper *illustration depicting the hangings at Gainesville, Texas. Although forty men were indeed hanged from the same elm, in truth they were executed only one and two at a time before being removed.*

for a favorable condition on the next Saturday, the day the jury was to meet."[29]

During the recess on Thursday, October 16, James A. Dickson, a well-known and prosperous Cooke County slaveholding resident, and two companions went out deer hunting in the cane breaks of Hickory Creek, along the Red River. During the outing they happened to see a man on horseback at the edge of a thicket and once he saw them he slowly rode off into a wooded area nearby. Curious, the men rode into the thicket to follow him but before reaching the woods, gunshots rang out and Dickson fell off his horse, mortally wounded. The other two immediately rode off in opposite directions to seek help.

One rider, a brother-in-law to Dickson, proceeded into Gainesville to report the shooting and to organize a posse to return. The other rider went to Col. William Young's nearby homestead and informed him of the

incident. Young quickly gathered a small band of men, including Col.
James Bourland, and proceeded to the ambush site.

Arriving in the area, Young's group was unable to locate Dickson's
body. The group from Gainesville had already arrived with a wagon and
were in the process of transporting it back to town. Riding further, Young
saw a group of horsemen and called out, thinking it was the Gainesville
group. They turned in their saddles and began firing, killing Colonel
Young, as his posse dismounted to seek cover to return fire. The other
horsemen, numbering between twenty to thirty, immediately rode off.

By the time Bourland and the others arrived back in Gainesville with
Young's body, they were convinced their assailants had been members of
the Union League.

"The excitement [had] boiled over," Barrett fretted, "[and] the situation
was fearful. I could discern the signs of the gathering storm by the expres-
sions of the crowd. . . . I spent my time in walking through the crowd and
hearing them talk, expecting every night the prison would be cleared."[29]

The attack on the Gainesville prison never came but the heated passions boiled over in Grayson County. Back in May 1861, the Sherman
Patriot office was broken into and vandals destroyed its press in an apparent
attempt to silence any efforts in forming a new Union state. By October
1862, however, the Unionist editor E. Junius Foster was back in full operation. Editorials condemning the Gainesville hangings had stirred indignation, but when he published an editorial proclaiming that William C.
Young's murder was one of the best things that had ever happened in North
Texas, it served only to accelerate a countdown on his life. Two nights later
three horsemen, years later determined to be James D. Young, William's
oldest son and former member of the 22nd Texas Cavalry, Newton J.
Chance, and an accomplice who was never identified, rode up behind Foster as he was locking the door of his print shop. Young demanded that Foster recant his statement about his father's death. Defiantly, Foster refused,
further adding that it was published because it was true. With that, Young
dismounted, rushed up and placed a double-barreled shotgun against Foster's side, and immediately discharged both barrels. Foster slowly died as the
three men rode away.[30]

The citizens' court reconvened on Saturday morning, October 18, but
three of the previously more moderate jurors who had opposed many of
the hangings failed to return. The court immediately replaced those vacan-

cies with Newton Chance, William W. Howeth, brother of guard Harvey Howeth who shot the escaping prisoners the previous week, and James W. McPherson, a trooper recruited off the street. Although Daniel Montague remained on the jury, he relinquished control as foreman, turning it over to Newt Chance.[31]

The deliberations began once more but this time based entirely on the transcripts of previous testimony. Most of these men had been implicated in earlier statements. No new information was presented. No witnesses or defendants were brought into the courtroom but Newt Chance continued to provide the jury with repeated renditions of what he knew.

"The testimony against the men," declared Barrett, "was all written down, consequently there was nothing to be done but read it, and take the vote."[32]

As the transcripts were read concerning each of the eighty men still in custody, the new reorganized jury, back to working again under the majority rule, simply voted to "set at liberty" or "hang." When a simple majority had condemned the first six men considered and the seventh was condemned on the barest of evidence, Barrett angrily chastised the jury and finally offered a compromise.

"I proposed to allow them to select six of the worst ones and hang them," he said, "and [to] set the rest at liberty."[33]

The jury rejected his idea but his outburst apparently served to restore some kind of order to the room and to break the dominating atmosphere of vengeance.

"There were nineteen men condemned to be hung," Barrett later noted, "[but] the balance, about fifty or sixty, were set at liberty."[34]

All nineteen executions were set for the next day, Sunday, October 19. Upon notification of their death sentence several of the condemned men tried to bargain for their lives, offering additional names, describing additional events, and providing additional details about various plans, none of which was of interest to the jury.

Early the next morning, Barrett and several others took their seats on the porch of the Foreman Hotel and watched as the "death wagon" shuttled the victims down the street to the hanging tree and the bodies back to the town square.

Capt. James D. Young, commanding a company of Partisan Rangers, guarded and escorted the wagon down to Pecan Creek and Young, himself,

Rounding up Unionists in the Gainesville, Texas, area as depicted in Frank Leslie's Illustrated Weekly Newspaper.

adjusted the noose around the neck of the first victim, thirty-eight-year-old John M. Crisp, a married blacksmith orignally from Kentucky. Twenty-four-year-old Richard N. Martin, married and originally from Wisconsin, made an angry, defiant speech to the crowd from the back of the death wagon before he was hanged, and Alexander D. Scott, a married thirty-nine year old farmer originally from Kentucky, was just as angry. Once the noose was adjusted around his neck and the wagon began to pull out from beneath the tree, A. D. Scott jumped from the bed, immediately breaking his own neck to spare himself the agony of strangulation. According to the witnesses, the hangings continued at the rate of two each hour until the sun went down.[35]

"[T]rials and hangings perpetually progress in all the counties," declared the Houston *Telegraph* not long after the events in Gainesville. "[T]he number of Unionists in Western and Northern Texas was small at first," the San Antonio *Herald* coldly observed a short time later, "and they are becoming every day less."[36]

Without a doubt, by the end of October 1862, Confederate control over the region had been undeniably established and any dissent had been silenced. Over a period of two and a half weeks, forty men had been hanged in addition to two being shot and killed trying to escape, at least one killed during the initial arrests, and an untold number murdered in various acts of violence throughout the eleven-county area. Lynchings in the surrounding counties followed those at Gainesville, causing many families to flee north into Federally controlled territory or south over the border into Mexico. Col. James G. Bourland and his troops showed no mercy as they crisscrossed the region in their patrols, executing draft dodgers, deserters, and suspected Unionists. So many complaints about murdered prisoners reached Gen. Henry McCulloch, Confederate commander of the Northern Sub-District of Texas, that he issued Colonel Bourland a reprimand and demanded a strict accounting of any future prisoner deaths. Bourland, however, eventually became known all across the region as "the hangman of Texas," and more than twenty men of his own command finally bolted, accused him of murder, and sought to initiate court-martial proceedings against him. Upon learning the details of the Gainesville hangings, Pres. Jefferson Davis, totally embarrassed by the development, dismissed Gen. Paul O. Hébert as military commander of Texas for "improper use of martial law" and abandoned his demand that the Union government conduct an official inquiry into the incident at Palmyra, Missouri.[37]

Chapter 5

"Dance the Damned Scoundrels . . . through Hell!"

SHELTON LAUREL

"The Rebels [Are] Carrying Out the Law of Retaliation," declared one banner headline of the *New York Times* in 1863. "President [Lincoln] has ordered that the stern law of retaliation shall without hesitation be enforced," declared yet another.[1]

As the beginning of 1863 dawned, Lincoln's Emancipation Proclamation went into effect, opening a Pandora's box of more atrocities and further retaliations. Shortly after black troops were mustered into Federal service many were executed as soon as they were captured. It occurred in Jasper County, Missouri, at Poison Springs, Arkansas, at Fort Pillow in Tennessee, at Milliken's Bend in Louisiana, and a number of places in North Carolina such as Plymouth, where captured black troops were lined up in groups along the Roanoke River and shot. But in the state of North Carolina, white Union troops were victimized as well.[2]

Like Missouri, loyalties in North Carolina were deeply divided. It was the last state to secede from the Union and did so only after Lincoln's demand for troops. A majority of its people originally wanted to stay out of the conflict and remain uncommitted until it became apparent military force would be used to bring the Southern states back into line. Although identifying strongly with the Union, under these circumstances many North Carolinians identified even more with the South and eventually the state provided nearly 125,000 Confederate troops, consisting of seventy-eight full regiments and nearly twenty battalions. By the end of the war nearly one-fifth of the entire Confederate army would be made up of those from North Carolina even though the state only had one-ninth of the total Southern population. But similar to Missouri, North Carolina possessed many isolated areas that remained deeply divided in their sentiments and eventually provided a number of Union troops as well. Such was the case in Madison County, thirty miles north of Asheville, bordering the state of Tennessee.

Located in the western part of the state, Madison was a rural mountainous county having high peaks and deep valleys. It was dotted with many small farms clinging to the sides of steep hills, with others tucked away in the gaps and coves, and on this rough and rocky land close-knit families scratched out a comfortable living raising a few livestock, corn, hay, and burley tobacco.

Many men of Madison County were members of the 64th North Carolina Volunteer Infantry. The core of this regiment began as Company A, Partisan Rangers, 11th Battalion, North Carolina Infantry, organized in May 1862. By the following July the battalion was increased to a full regiment and designated the 64th. Lawrence M. Allen, a twenty-nine-year-old, fairly wealthy landowner and speculator of Madison County who owned two servants, became colonel of the regiment. Allen, married with three children, was involved in local politics, having served as clerk of the county's superior court for a number of years, and becoming a high-ranking member of the Democratic party.

"Colonel Allen," offered Capt. B. T. Morris, Co. A, 64th North Carolina, "was not an attractive man—rather otherwise—but was chosen leader because he was known to be brave and fearless. Fighting was expected, and his men had the utmost confidence in him."[3]

Allen's thirty-eight-year-old cousin, James A. Keith, a physician of Mars Hill, Madison County, became second in command upon being promoted from captain of the Partisan Rangers to lieutenant colonel of the 64th. Keith, also married with two children, had prior military experience as a soldier in the Mexican War. He also had two servants and was one of the twenty wealthiest men of Madison County.[4]

In fact, six full companies of men in this regiment were from Madison County with the other four being a company from Henderson, another from Polk, and two from nearby counties of Tennessee.[5]

Still, there were other residents of Madison County who were pro-Union, and they had either stayed out of the service altogether or had ventured over the border to nearby Greeneville or Knoxville, Tennessee, to join Union regiments being formed there, units that were eventually designated the 1st Tennessee Cavalry Regiment and the 2nd Tennessee Cavalry Regiment. Still others organized in those cities a year later were designated the 2nd Regiment North Carolina Mounted Infantry and the 3rd Regiment North Carolina Mounted Infantry. After the forming of each, a number of Madison County men deserted the Confederate 64th North Carolina and joined friends or family in the Union regiments. The most widely known and influential throughout Madison County, North Carolina, as well as Greene County, Tennessee, in these regiments were the Kirk brothers of Company I, 1st Tennessee (Union) Cavalry Regiment. These men, George, John, James, Francis, and William were farmers in the Greeneville area. John L. Kirk enlisted with his older brother, George, in August 1862, and eventually reached the rank of captain, while brother George W. Kirk would eventually go on to serve in the 2nd North Carolina (Union) Mounted Infantry and, still later, become colonel of the 3rd North Carolina (Union) Mounted Infantry.

The 1st Tennessee was originally organized at Camp Garber, Flat Lick, Kentucky, about twenty miles northwest of the Cumberland Gap, in April 1862. The regiment was made up of men mostly from Knox County, Kentucky, and Greene, Cocke, Bradley, and Knox counties in Tennessee. Company I of that regiment was organized the following August and included only men from the Tennessee counties of Bradley and Greene, including the Kirk brothers.

All of these regiments, both Union and Confederate, eventually operated in and around western North Carolina and eastern Tennessee for most of the war. By January 1863, the war had created an economic hardship in this region. Most of the men were away at war and roving bands of foraging troops, including Union, Confederate, a number of partisan units, and marauders, had each taken their toll. Food had become scarce and salt was one of the more serious shortages. It was essential in preserving meat and preventing spoilage for home use as well as army rations. At the beginning of the war the price of salt averaged $12 for a two-bushel sack. When the price of salt reached $100 a sack in North Carolina during the war, Gov. Zebulon B.Vance established the office of salt commissioner in an effort to

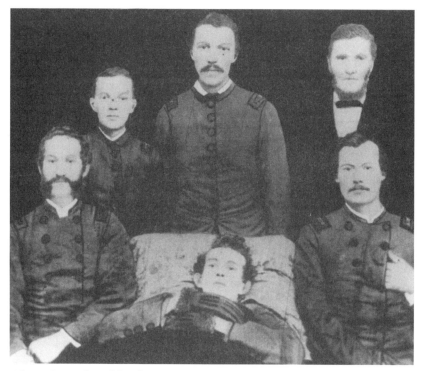

Alexander Kirk and his five Union sons. John L. Kirk, leader of the raid in Marshall, North Carolina, is at the front left of the photo. The others, clockwise, are Francis M. Kirk, James F. Kirk, father Alexander Kirk, Col. George W. Kirk, and Capt. William H. Kirk, bedridden in this photo due to the recent amputation of his leg. Leon S. Kirk Collection at USAMHI

stabilize the rising cost and to regulate the sale and distribution of the commodity. He stepped in again in late 1862 and placed an embargo on the export of salt from the state. As part of these regulatory efforts, all salt supplies were seized and held for rationing by the Confederate authorities.[6]

But government intervention simply added to the salt famine. The commodity became so scarce that many local salt commissioners resigned out of fear of the increasing danger of having such a position. The local authorities had created additional problems by distributing salt rations only to the local citizens who sympathized with the Confederacy while withholding it from the families of all known or suspected Union sympathizers. This latter group consisted of many anxious families in the Shelton Laurel community, many of whom had postponed their yearly winter hog slaughterings because of the scarcity of the salt needed for curing and preserving the meat. By January 1863, salt, some food items, and other necessities were in increasingly short supply. With the severity of midwinter setting in, conditions for some families in this region were becoming quite desperate.[7]

During the night of January 8, 1863, about fifty men rode into Marshall, North Carolina, from several different directions. It was common knowledge that the Confederacy maintained a supply depot in the town of Marshall, the Madison County seat, and that it included plenty of salt.

Capt. John Peek, Co. C, 64th North Carolina Volunteer Infantry, Col. Lawrence Allen's brother-in-law, was home on leave at the time and was asleep at his house on Main Street. Upon being awakened by loud voices and strange noises, he went to investigate. Just as he emerged from his doorway his right arm was shattered by a gunshot as he discovered Union soldiers and civilian raiders plundering the storehouse. The leader of the group, wearing a Federal uniform, was recognized as John L. Kirk, Company I, 1st Tennessee (Union) Cavalry Regiment. Although a number were in Federal uniforms, others were in civilian clothes and some of them were identified as having deserted or once served in the 64th North Carolina Confederate Regiment.[8]

Additional shots were fired but Peek remained the raid's only casualty as more witnesses arrived on the scene but stayed out of sight. The raiders moved on to Lawrence Allen's house farther down on Main Street and terrorized his wife, children, and servants. Locked closets and trunks were broken into and a number of items were taken. As the regiment rode out of town several more homes were broken into and ransacked. Authorities later determined that about fifty bushels of salt, large batches of cotton gauze, and an unspecified number of blankets and clothing were taken from the Confederate storehouse while additional food, clothing, blankets, money, and several horses and mules were taken from the individual homes along the escape route.[9]

"The attack on Marshall," reported Confederate brigadier general William G. M. Davis, brigade commander, Department of East Tennessee, stationed at Knoxville, "has given rise to wild rumors of organizations of armed [Unionists] throughout the mountains, bent on sacking towns and the plunder of loyal men."[10]

Colonel Allen, in Knoxville awaiting disposition of several previous charges filed against him, learned of the raid three days later. He had been

Brig. Gen. Henry Heth, Confederate commander of the Department of East Tennessee, was furious and fed up with the recurring problems in the east Tennessee-western North Carolina area and ordered his troops to "clean out the insurrectionary country." NATIONAL ARCHIVES

relieved of duty and suspended without pay for six months back in January 1862 for filing a false report and recruiting irregularities and had been charged again with "crime and drunkenness" before the suspension had ended. Upon hearing his family had been victimized, Allen assumed command of Captain Thomas M. Nelson's Independent Company of Partisan Rangers, Georgia Cavalry, stationed at Knoxville, drew supplies and rations, and headed out toward Greeneville with them apparently without consulting with Brig. Gen. Henry Heth, his Confederate commander in the Department of East Tennessee. At about the same time Lieutenant Colonel Keith, in command of the 64th North Carolina in Allen's absence, and stationed at Strawberry Plains, Tennessee, where detachments of the 64th were guarding a railroad bridge, learned of the Marshall raid and headed out toward Knoxville, a distance of eighteen miles, to confer with Heth.

Keith found Brigadier General Heth furious and fed up with the recurring problems in the east Tennessee–North Carolina region. He ordered Keith to take 200 of his men stationed at Strawberry Plains with another 25 at Greeneville, where an additional company of cavalry would join him, and proceed into the Laurel valley to clean out the "insurrectionary country."

Gathering his troops at Strawberry Plains and proceeding on to Greeneville, Keith discovered the company of cavalry that General Heth had promised was Nelson's and it was now under the command of Allen. Although Keith protested, stating he had been placed in their command, Allen rode out of town in command of the unit. Keith and the 64th North Carolina Regiment headed out toward North Carolina on a different route. On January 15 the two Confederate columns rode into the Laurel valley separately but united in their purpose.

Bordered by the Bald Mountains of the Appalachians, the valley was named for the abundance of mountain laurel in the vicinity and the fact the Shelton brothers were its first settlers in the 1790s. The valley floor is naturally divided by three swift running streams: Big Laurel Creek, Little Laurel Creek, and Shelton Laurel Creek. The community of Shelton Laurel, consisting merely of a number of self-sufficient farm homes but no businesses, was located about ten miles north of Marshall. Colonel Allen reached Shelton Laurel a day ahead of Keith and set up a command post. Summoning Keith the next day, the two met and agreed they needed to work together because firm action was necessary to "suppress the insurrection." By that afternoon, Friday, January 16, their squads had fanned out all across the valley to "arrest any male citizens" in the vicinity.

"I hope you will not relax until the [Unionists] are crushed," cautioned Governor Vance of North Carolina. "But do not let our excited people deal too harshly with these misguided men."[11]

Over the next two days about twenty Shelton Laurel males were taken into custody. One cavalry unit captured four and turned them over to Adj. Gen. W. H. Bailey. These men, Sipus Shelton and his son David, Isaac Shelton, and William Morton, were escorted to Asheville for incarceration. Meanwhile, Allen and Keith's troops were conducting "interrogations" throughout the community.

"You will see that no injury is done to the persons or property of peaceable citizens," Colonel Allen had been instructed by Asst. Adj. Gen. Charles S. Stringer three months earlier while conducting similar operations in Kentucky and east Tennessee. "Citizens known to be of Union sentiments but engaging in no act of hostility will not be molested."[12]

Apparently Allen decided those rules no longer applied now that he was in North Carolina. His troops rode up to the home of sixty-eight-year-old Unus Riddle and began asking questions. When she refused to answer some of their inquiries, they dragged her out into the yard and whipped her. When she still refused, a rope was thrown over her head and draped over a nearby tree branch and she was hoisted into the air repeatedly. While this "interview" was taking place, other soldiers searched her house and robbed her of a considerable amount of money. Allen and Keith next led their troops on to the home of twenty-six-year-old Sarah Shelton, wife of Ezra Shelton, who apparently had been involved in the Marshall raid but had quickly fled the area when the Confederate troops first came into the valley. Sarah, too, was whipped and threatened and a noose thrown over her head until she confessed all she knew about the raid and the whereabouts of any participants. The soldiers then moved on to the home of Sallie Moore, fifty-five, dragged her out into the yard and whipped her and proceeded to do the same to a number of women throughout the Shelton Laurel valley. During these forays Allen and Keith's troops recovered a number of items and rounded up sixteen males found hiding in the area. Martha Shelton's husband James, thirty-six, and their two other sons, James Jr., sixteen, and David, thirteen, were taken into custody as well as Roderick "Stob Rod" Shelton, forty-eight, and his brother David Shelton, forty; Azariah Shelton, seventeen; William Shelton, twenty-one; Julius Halen Moore, twenty-three; Henry Wade Moore, eighteen; James Metcalf, thirty-nine; Ellison King, twenty-four; Joseph Woods, sixty; Jasper M. Chandler, eighteen; John Norton, fourteen; Peter McCoy, twenty-one; and Joseph Clendennon, fourteen. They were all taken to the Judith Shelton cabin, a large hewed-log structure located in the Laurel Creek bottoms, and confined in a large front room with a guard posted at each door.[13]

During the night of January 18, Peter McCoy attacked one of the guards, hit him with a rock, and escaped. The next morning as guards rousted the prisoners out of the house John Norton hid under a bed and went unnoticed. A squad of eight soldiers under the command of Sgt. Nicholas B. D. Jay, a Virginian attached to Company K of the 64th Regiment, accompanied by Lt. R. M. Deaver of Company F, and, according to some reports, a number of Madison County men from Company A including Pvts. Jacob C. Ramsey, Ned Ramsey, John Ramsey, Solomon M. Carter, G. W. Higgins, James Moore Ray, William "Shelt" Ray, and Joseph "Tyler" Ray and, in still other reports, including Maj. William M. Garrett and Lt. Col. James Keith, escorted the prisoners down the lane away from the house. Many of the captives insisted they were innocent, claiming they had not been in on the Marshall raid. Someone in the military escort replied that they would have the opportunity to prove that in front of a military commission at Knoxville. Not mentioned was the fact several of these captives were known to have previously deserted the 64th North Carolina Regiment. James M. Shelton was once a member of Co. C, having joined in July 1861. H. Wade Moore and his cousin J. Halen Moore, as well as William Shelton and Roderick Shelton, had originally been members of Co. A of the 64th, having joined on May 10, 1862, and then apparently transferred to Co. F the following July when Ellison King, James Metcalf, and Joseph Wood enlisted in Co. F in July 1862. That same July Jasper M. Chandler had enlisted in Co. E and David Shelton had been in Co. M, having joined on September 1, 1862. On November 25 they had all deserted from their various companies and although there were a few Sheltons from North Carolina enlisted in Co. I of the 1st Tennessee Union regiment, none of them were any of the men now in custody.[14]

Perhaps these prisoners thought about those previous desertions as they were pushed and prodded along the lane. Surely they knew some of their captors. After all, Keith had been captain of Company A when the Moores and William and Roderick Shelton had first enlisted, and all three companies of the 64th that had left Strawberry Plains to serve on the Shelton Laurel mission, companies A, C, and D, were made up entirely of Madison County men. But more probably these prisoners couldn't help but think about their families they were leaving behind. Most of this group of captives who weren't mere boys were married with children of their own. Aside from two of his children being with him, James Shelton had four more children back home. The elder David Shelton was married with six small children. His brother Roderick also had six small children, William Shelton was married with two, and James Metcalf was married with one—a three-year-old child—back home.[15]

Did these thoughts play upon many of the prisoners' minds as they were ordered to turn northwest off the roadway, about two miles southwest of the Judith Shelton cabin, where the Hickey Fork stream runs into Shelton Laurel Creek? The captives were marched down into a forested hollow, several hundred feet off the roadway, and ordered to halt and then to kneel.

"For God's sake," remarked prisoner Joseph Wood, "you're not going to shoot us?"[16]

Immediately an order was given to "fire" and five prisoners fell over as the soldiers quickly moved over to the next five prisoners down on their knees and shot them as well. By the time the troopers had moved over to the four remaining captives, thirteen-year-old David Shelton was pleading for his life but four more shots rang out and echoed down through the timber. Having noticed one prisoner still struggling, a trooper walked over and casually shot the man in the head. Afterwards, the lifeless bodies were dragged over to a nearby eroded ditch and rolled in. Gleefully, Sergeant Jay ran over and began jumping up and down on the bodies as he yelled "Pat Juba for me while I dance the damned scoundrels down into and through hell!"[17]

Once the soldiers had left, nearby resident George "Rock" Franklin loaded the dead bodies onto an oxen-drawn sled and hauled them back to the Judith Shelton's cabin where they were buried in a common grave near Huckleberry Knob.

When the Confederate troops arrived back in Greeneville on January 20, 1863, Captain Nelson reported that his rangers had killed twelve men and captured twenty in various engagements in the Shelton valley. Colonel Keith reported his troops had met strong resistance in the area and had killed several they had tried to capture. In fact, Confederate military authorities apparently began adding notations on several of the men's military records to cover their actions. "Absent without leave—On sick furlough, time expired and then joined a band of robbers," they noted on Henry Wade Moore's record, "and was killed in arms against C[onfererate] S[tates] in Madison County, NC." Curiously, shortly afterward, according to military records, Pvt. G. W. Higgins deserted in "Laurell, NC," on February 10. Solomon Carter went home "sick" the following March and never returned to his regiment while Joseph T. Ray deserted on March 24 and James M. Ray resigned the following August.[18]

Meanwhile, several weeks passed before North Carolina's governor learned of the appalling details regarding the Shelton Laurel operation. In mid-February he sent Asheville prosecutor Augustus S. Merrimon to investigate.

"Most of them were taken at their homes and none of them made resistance when taken," reported Merrimon. "The prisoners were captured on one Friday and killed the next Monday [and] several women were severely whipped and ropes were tied around their necks."[19]

Upon learning that Lt. Col. James A. Keith was in command of the troops and had ordered the execution, Governor Vance demanded action of Confederate Secretary of War James A. Seddon.

The mass grave on Huckleberry Knob, Shelton Laurel, North Carolina, as it appears today. LONNIE R. SPEER

"I desire you to have proceedings instituted at once against this offi-cer," wrote Vance, "who, if the half be true, is a disgrace to the service and to North Carolina."[20]

Colonel Allen denied any knowledge of these executions. He admitted to having been present during the floggings of the women but had been at his home in Marshall, grieving over the recent death of his son from scarlet fever and near death of his daughter, when the prisoners were removed from their confinement. Colonel Keith, on the other hand, never denied his involvement but claimed he did so because of "verbal" orders given to him by General Heth during their Knoxville meeting, which stated in part, "he did not want to be troubled with prisoners" and that "the last one of them ought to be killed," referring to the Unionists in that part of the county.[21]

"[T]he prisoners were shot," Keith admitted, "but the shooting was considered a military necessity and absolutely necessary to protect the loyal citizens of that country . . . as to whipping the women, I can only say that I did order these women whipped [and] I succeeded in recovering about 50 bunches of cotton gauze, about 30 bushels of salt, and a large quantity of wearing apparel."[22]

In the following weeks Governor Vance continued to pressure Seddon to take some kind of action against those responsible. Meanwhile the event gained more and more publicity.

"Sergeant N.B.D. Jay, of Capt. Reynolds' company, and Lieutenant R. M. Deaver assisted their men in the execution of these hellish outrages," reported the *Memphis Bulletin* and then the *New York Times* as knowledge of the Shelton Laurel incident reached beyond the Appalachian Mountains to gain national attention. Eventually, the "outrages" of the American Civil War reached Europe as Germany's *Westliche Post* reported "[T]he terrible execution of Union men by the rebel Colonel Keith, who must be a monster, as he spares neither age nor infancy."[23]

Finally, on April 26, 1863, "in the interest of the service" Colonel Keith and four junior officers turned in their resignations and were allowed to resign. Colonel Allen's resignation was requested soon afterwards. Gen. Henry Heth, implicated by Keith and two others, but said to have been the only general in the Confederate service that Gen. Robert E. Lee commonly

The "forested hollow" on the northwest side of Shelton Laurel Creek at Hickey Fork where the Shelton Laurel executions took place, as it appears today.

LONNIE R. SPEER

referred to by his first name, was transferred to the Army of Northern Virginia at Lee's request, promoted to major general, placed in command of a division in the III Corps, and later served under A. P. Hill at Gettysburg.

"[Heth] admits that he told Keith that those found in arms ought not be treated as enemies," Seddon advised Governor Vance after his investigation, " and in the event of an engagement . . . to take no prisoners . . . but he denies in strong terms the making use of any remarks which would authorize maltreatment of prisoners who had been accepted as such."[24]

Similar to the situation involving Union general John McNeil in Missouri, everyone responsible for North Carolina's incident escaped culpability. Due to more pressing matters, the Confederacy had no further interests in pursuing an investigation, leaving those in Shelton Laurel even more isolated and more deeply divided in their sentiments for years to come.

Chapter 6

"I Regret I Did Not Burn Any Bridges"

CORBIN AND McGRAW

Like Missouri, north Texas, North Carolina, and Tennessee, Kentucky was deeply divided in its loyalties. A native state to both Abraham Lincoln and Jefferson Davis, Kentucky was strongly nationalistic but economically Southern. When Gov. George W. Johnson refused to heed Lincoln's call for troops and the state legislature voted to remain neutral, Kentuckians were promised Federal troops would never cross its borders as long as the state remained peaceful. Still, many of its citizens volunteered for military service. Union recruits enlisted at camps north of the Ohio River while Confederate recruits enlisted in camps just over the border in Tennessee and Virginia. Eventually, nearly 76,000 Kentuckians served in the Union army while at the same time about 25,000 served with the Confederate forces. But feelings were so divided in the state that, in some cases, homeguard units of individual communities often formed two different organizations—one pro-Union and one pro-Confederate.[1]

With such passionate feelings it was no surprise that the state's neutrality didn't last long. Within a month Lincoln violated his own agreement and declared that Unionists in Kentucky would be given aid, and then in July he advised that his War Department would actively canvass both Kentucky and Tennessee for volunteers. In response, Confederate forces entered Kentucky from Tennessee the following September and took the cities of Hickman and Columbus while Union forces countered by taking the city of Paducah. Minor engagements followed all across the state during the remainder of the year but by February 1862, the state was, by and large, under Union control. Still, Southern sympathies remained throughout the region for quite some time, causing minor irritation to the Union authorities.[2]

"[A]ll persons found within our lines who commit acts for the benefit of the enemies of our country will be tried as spies or traitors and if convicted will suffer death," declared General Orders No. 38 issued on April 13, 1863, by Union major general Ambrose E. Burnside, Union commander of the Department of the Ohio.[3]

According to Major General Burnside's order, acts benefiting the enemy included carrying or delivering secret mail, writers of letters sent by secret mail, enemy recruiting officers behind or within Union lines, people who crossed Union lines for the purpose of enlisting with the enemy, people found concealed within Union lines belonging to the service of the enemy or providing information to the enemy, and all people within Union lines who harbored, protected, concealed, fed, clothed, or in any way aided the enemy. "It must be distinctly understood," Burnside warned in Orders No. 38, "that treason expressed or implied will not be tolerated in this department [and] the habit of declaring sympathies for the enemy will not be allowed."[4]

Four days earlier, Capt. William F. Corbin and his friend, Pvt. T. Jefferson McGraw, both of Co. D, 4th Kentucky (Confederate) Cavalry, were at Rouse's Mill, in Pendleton County, Kentucky, actively, but secretly, recruiting for the Confederate army. Dressed in civilian clothes, Corbin had a recruiting commission from Confederate authorities signed by Brig. Gen. Humphrey Marshall, 1st Brigade, Army of East Tennessee, headquartered in Abingdon, Virginia.[5]

Corbin and McGraw were preparing to return to the Confederate-held territory on the other side of the border with seven men whom they had enlisted when they were captured by Union troops. Corbin, age thirty, was apprehended wearing a Colt revolver, a large knife, and having Confederate letters concealed on him along with the signed recruiting commission. McGraw, age thirty-three, was wearing a Colt revolver and carrying a Confederate-issued musket. Placed under arrest as spies, they were escorted the forty miles to Burnside's headquarters at Cincinnati, Ohio, for incarceration.[6]

Capt. William F. Corbin, Co. D, 4th Kentucky Cavalry, executed at Johnson's Island along with T. Jefferson McGraw. CONFEDERATE VETERAN

In truth, Union authorities had long held that Confederate soldiers apprehended in civilian attire behind the lines were to be treated as spies and suffer accordingly, but it was never officially declared policy in this area. By all appearances, the Department of Ohio's General Orders No. 38, issued four days later to encompass the state of Kentucky, was issued by Major General Burnside as a result of these arrests.[7]

On April 22, 1863, nine days after the Order was issued and approximately two weeks after the arrests, the defendants were brought before a military commission convened in Cincinnati under the direction of Brig. Gen. Robert B. Potter, U.S. Volunteers, for courts-martial. Corbin was charged with two crimes—recruiting men within the lines of U.S. forces and being a carrier of mails from within U.S. lines to persons in arms against the U.S. Government—to which he pleaded "not guilty." During the trial additional evidence surfaced indicating that Corbin had also been involved in burning several bridges on the Kentucky Central Railroad. Thomas Jefferson McGraw was brought up next, simply charged with recruiting men within the lines of the U.S. forces. When asked how he pled, he defiantly responded, "I regret I did not burn any bridges!"[8]

Needless to say, such a defiant attitude didn't help their situation. Within two days, both men were found guilty of all charges and sentenced to be shot.

"The proceedings, findings and sentences in the foregoing cases are approved and confirmed," declared Burnside. "The prisoners, William F. Corbin and T. J. McGraw, now or late of the so-called Confederate Army, will be sent in irons by the proper officer and delivered into the custody of the commanding officer on Johnson's Island, depot of prisoners of war, near Sandusky, Ohio. The commanding officer of that post will see that the sentences are duly executed at that post between the hours of 12 o'clock noon and 3 o'clock p.m. of Friday, May 15, 1863. Subject to the approval of the President of the United States."[9]

"The following instructions for the government of armies of the United States in the field," announced General Orders No. 100, officially issued by the U.S. War Department on April 24 in an apparent attempt to cover their tracks, "prepared by Francis Lieber, LL. D., and revised by a board of officers of which Maj. Gen. E. A. Hitchcock is president, having been approved by the President of the United States, [and of which] he commands that they be published for the information of all concerned," defined the rules of war according to the Union government including the definition of spies, their apprehension, and punishment.[10]

Ten days later the cases of Corbin and McGraw were presented to President Lincoln for his review. Apparently ignoring the fact that Orders No. 38 covering the state of Kentucky was issued four days after their arrest and that Orders No. 100, officially specifying what action would be taken in such cases, was issued after their trials had ended, he endorsed the executions. "The foregoing sentence is approved," he wrote, and then signed it: "May 4, 1863. A. Lincoln."[11]

Heavily shackled, Corbin and McGraw were transported by train to Sandusky where they were placed on the *Little Eastern,* a small steamboat that transported prisoners from the mainland to the island. Once it docked at the Johnson's Island wharf, the prison commandant, Maj. William S. Pierson, a Yale graduate and former mayor of Sandusky, along with Lt. George Hollenbeck, acting provost marshal, and a guard unit under the command of Capt. Thomas H. Linnell, took charge of the prisoners and escorted them the short distance to the prison.

Being a major Union POW facility, and the only prison actually built specifically for holding prisoners of war, Johnson's Island Military Prison had separate accommodations for housing condemned men awaiting formal execution. Two small square buildings, located several hundred yards from the general prison barracks but still within the compound, stood in the southeast corner. Both buildings were divided into eight small rooms, each about seven feet high, two and a half feet wide, and just long enough to lie down in. A little window, about six inches by one and a half inches, admitted the only light and fresh air. Each condemned prisoner was required to wear a sixty-four-pound ball connected to a six-foot chain, which was attached to one leg with the shackle riveted around the ankle. Handcuffs secured the prisoner's wrists in front of him at all times. During the day, under guard, the prisoner was allowed to sling the ball over his shoulder and walk around within a staked off area of about fifteen square feet in front of the building for exercise. At sunset, each condemned prisoner was locked up separately in his assigned compartment.[13]

These prisoners were guarded by special details drawn from the Hoffman Battalion, a Sandusky unit that was recruited and trained specifically to guard POWs—the only one of its kind in the entire Civil War. When Corbin and McGraw arrived, seven of those sixteen rooms were already occupied by others who had been sentenced to death and six of those were men from Kentucky. George P. Simms and William S. Burgess had been arrested as "spies" at Ruggles' Mills, Kentucky, nearly ten days after Corbin and McGraw, and were awaiting their sentence to be hanged on May 29. They, too, had been recruiting. Also incarcerated were John R. Lyle, arrested for recruiting in Bowling Green and sentenced to hang on May 27; John Marr, arrested in Paris, Kentucky, as a spy on April 5 and also sentenced to hang on May 29 with Simms and Burgess; H. P. Esteph, Co. H, 14th Kentucky, arrested as a spy on April 1, 1863, and sentenced to be hanged; and Thomas M. Campbell, arrested as a spy at Ruggles' Mills as well. Campbell, Co. I, 2nd Independent Kentucky Regiment, arrested on April 11, had been sentenced to hang on May 1 but had recently received a reprieve until May 8. Also incarcerated in one of the rooms was a Union deserter, John C. Shore, Co. F, 109th Illinois Infantry, sentenced to be shot. Although Corbin and McGraw's arrival increased the prison's condemned population to an all-time high of nine, its general population was

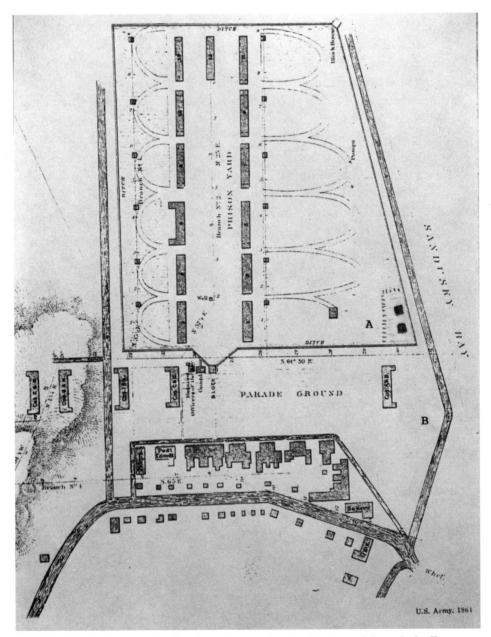

Sketch of Johnson's Island Military Prison showing location of the staked-off prison guardhouses (A) used to house the condemned and the location (B) where the official executions took place. AUTHOR'S COLLECTION

quite low when they arrived. Due to a temporary exchange agreement with the Confederacy, the total number being held in the prison had been drastically reduced to only forty.[13]

During the following days the only opportunity the two prisoners had to see and talk to each other was during their exercise periods. As the day of their execution approached, Corbin and McGraw, learning of new developments involving other prisoners while in the exercise yard, possibly entertained some hope. On May 7 Campbell's execution was again postponed, this time to May 21, as President Lincoln reviewed the case. Cautiously, Corbin and McGraw gained some confidence, or at least hope, of a reprieve of their own as their execution date grew near. They were aware that Corbin's close friend, J. C. DeMoss, was aiding Corbin's sister in seeking the help of several prominent Union men in Kentucky on their behalf. Meanwhile, Major Pierson began his preparations for the approaching event.

"I received your dispatch in which you direct no visitors on the island the day of execution," he acknowledged in correspondence with Col. William Hoffman, Union commissary general of prisoners, "[but the] doctor [post physician Dr. Timothy Woodbridge] desires Doctor Donahoe [of Sandusky] and perhaps another physician," admitted Pierson. "The chaplain [Rev. Robert McCune] said he would like another clergyman, [and] I also consented that the sheriff of one county (Sandusky) be present as I am under obligations to him for irons, etc., besides [he] being very accommodating in taking prisoners sometimes in the winter. I also design to give passes to reporters of the press. . . . These executions make very great excitement in the northern part of Ohio."[14]

Pierson's requests were approved as Corbin and McGraw awaited their reprieve. Miss Corbin, finding no help among Union acquaintances, went to General Burnside in Cincinnati and made an appeal but was told there would be no recommendation of clemency in the case. She and DeMoss then proceeded to Washington, D.C., to contact President Lincoln but he refused to meet with them. Next, they appealed to Rev. Dr. Byron Sunderland, a well-known Presbyterian minister of Washington who was personally acquainted with Lincoln. Sunderland approached the President in their behalf but was told there would be no reprieve in this case because the men were "bridge-burners."[15]

On the morning of May 15, access to the island was restricted to only the military, the press, and the few civilians Pierson had requested. The general prison population was confined to close quarters and the island was picketed throughout. General Burnside was also present with his staff.

Corbin's close friend, J. Calvin DeMoss of Flagg Spring, Kentucky, was allowed on the island to help comfort the men and accompanied the two as they were escorted to the prison chapel by guards and the prison chaplains.

"After reading and prayer," recalled DeMoss, "Captain Corbin said, speaking of himself, that life was just as sweet to him as to any man; he was ready to die, and did not fear death; he had done nothing he was ashamed of, but had acted on his own convictions, and was not sorry for what he had done; he was fighting for a principle, which in the sight of God and man, and in the view of death which awaited him, he believed was right, and, feeling this, he had nothing to fear."[16]

McGraw, too, faced death fearlessly. "I . . . leave a mother, two sisters, a brother, and friends to mourn my loss," he solemnly remarked.[17]

At about 1:00 P.M. the Hoffman battalion, under the command of Captain Linnell, marched to a site outside of the prison on the south side of the island. Here, fronting the bay, they formed a hollow square open on the bay side. Twenty minutes later a two-horsedrawn government wagon slowly approached the area, heavily flanked by a military guard escort and followed by the post band playing the "Dead March." Corbin and Mc-Graw, securely manacled and shackled and seated upon their own coffins, rode in the bed of the wagon, with Reverend McCune between them.[18]

Once they arrived at the designated spot, the pine coffins were dragged off the wagon and along the shore to the center of the square and the prisoners took their seats upon them, facing a sixteen-guard execution squad. Major Pierson, along with his staff and friends, took a position on the right as Adjutant Bailey stepped forward and read the charges and sentence against the two prisoners.

"Hope [for a reprieve] was maintained until the last," recalled J. C. DeMoss, "and the officers in charge at Johnson's [Island] delayed the execution until the last moment."[19]

"I am desired by these unfortunate men to return their thanks to the Commander of this post and to all officers and men with whom they have had intercourse, for the kindness and sympathy they have received since their arrival here," declared Reverend McCune as he stood beside Corbin and McGraw. "I am also charged by them to say to all in attendance that they die forgiving all enemies and accusers, and in love and charity with all

A typical military execution by firing squad during the Civil War as depicted in Harper's Weekly.

men, believing in the Gospel of Jesus Christ, and that they have been thus far consoled and sustained by its truth and that, trusting in the mercy of God through Christ, they have good hope of eternal life."[20]

The crowd remained hushed as McCune recited a prayer. Once completed, military personnel solemnly stepped forward, pulled hoods down over the heads of Corbin and McGraw, and stepped back into line. The next few moments seemed like an eternity to everyone present. Finally, the silence was broken by Lieutenant Hollenbeck: "READY! . . . AIM! . . . FIRE!"[21]

"The firing was instantaneous," reported the Sandusky *Commercial Register,* "so that the sixteen muskets seemed to make but one report. The men both fell back upon their coffins and died without a struggle. Corbin did not move a muscle—McGraw gasped twice."[22]

After examination by physicians, both men were pronounced dead. The battalion lined up and coldly marched past the bodies to the "Dead

March" as they returned to the parade ground for dismissal. General Burnside stepped forward and turned the bodies over to DeMoss for their return to Kentucky for burial.

Corbin's and McGraw's pending executions had become a focal point in a dispute between the two governments over the status of officers found recruiting behind enemy lines. Richmond authorities refused to accept the Union position that recruiting behind the lines was a form of espionage but, even with that, had failed to come to the two men's aid politically, or otherwise, before the executions were carried out. The delay by officials in Richmond probably cost the two men their lives. Unfortunately for Corbin and McGraw, Confederate authorities were preoccupied at the time coping with the recent death of Gen. "Stonewall" Jackson.

Chapter 7

"So Shall We Do by Lee"

FLINN AND SAWYER, AND LEE

"I perceive by the Northern papers that Captains [*sic*] McGraw and Corbin were shot to death with musketry on Friday," complained Robert Ould, Confederate agent of prisoner exchange, in a dispatch directed at Lt. Col. William H. Ludlow, Union agent of exchange, days after Stonewall Jackson's funeral. "These men were duly authorized to recruit within the limits of Kentucky . . . [therefore] [t]he Confederate Government has ordered that two captains now in our custody shall be selected for execution in retaliation for this gross barbarity."[1]

"I give you formal notice," Ludlow angrily responded, "that for each officer so executed, one of your officers in our hands will be immediately put to death and if this number be not sufficient it will be increased."[2]

"Your papers refer to other cases of parties condemned to death upon the same charge [as Corbin and McGraw]," Ould continued. "They are some five or six in number. In view of the awful vortex into which things are plunging I give you notice that in the event of the execution of these persons retaliation to an equal extent at least will be visited upon your own officers, and if that is found ineffectual the number will be increased."[3]

"By your own admission," Ludlow argued, "your officers and men have come within our lines for the purpose ostensibly of recruiting but really as spies. They have been taken in citizens' dress under all the circumstances clearly surrounding the character of a spy. And in accepting such service they have taken upon themselves all its responsibility and the consequence of capture."[4]

Were it not for the fact Ould and Ludlow were wagering the lives of actual human beings, their heated exchanges of May 1863 would seem almost childish. But regardless of Ludlow's threats for continued retaliation if necessary, President Lincoln was unwilling to test the Confederates. On May 21 Lincoln gave Thomas M. Campbell, the Johnson Island prisoner originally scheduled for execution before Corbin and McGraw, a reprieve and had him returned to the general prison population. On May 25, two days before the prison's next scheduled execution, Lincoln suspended the death sentence of the prisoner, John R. Lyle, and did the same regarding the executions of Simms, Burgess, and Marr, scheduled for May 29.[5]

In spite of Lincoln's efforts to end the controversy over the possibility of retaliation, Confederate officials remained infuriated over Ludlow's posture. Southern prison officials arbitrarily chose Capt. Samuel McKee, 14th Kentucky (Union) Cavalry, and Capt. E. A. Sheppard, 5th New York Cavalry, both being held in Richmond's Libby Prison, for retaliation in the deaths of Corbin and McGraw. McKee and Sheppard both had influential Southern ties, however, and those friends began a letter-writing campaign in their behalf on May 30. Within two weeks both men were removed from isolation and turned back into the general prison population as Confederate authorities considered some other alternative.[6]

"[Y]our officers in different districts have recently taken the lives of prisoners who fell into their power and justify their act by asserting a right to treat as spies the military officers and enlisted men under my command," Jefferson Davis complained in a dispatch to Abraham Lincoln. "I have heretofore on different occasions been forced to make complaints of these outrages, and to ask from you that you should either avow or disclaim having authorized them, and have failed to obtain such answer. . . . [T]hese usages justify and indeed require redress by retaliation as the proper means of repressing such cruelties . . . [I therefore make] one last solemn attempt to avert such calamities and to attest my earnest desire to prevent them if it be possible."[7]

Lincoln did not directly respond to Davis but soon after issued General Order No. 252, which proclaimed, in part, "for every soldier of the United States killed in violation of the laws of war a rebel soldier shall be executed."[8]

On July 6 Capt. Thomas P. Turner, prison commandant, and his entourage entered Libby Prison with an official order signed by Brig. Gen. John H. Winder, Richmond's commissary general of prisoners.

"Captain T. P. Turner, Commanding Confederate States Prison, " read Special Orders No. 160, "is hereby directed to select by lot from among the Federal captains now in his custody, two of that number for execution."[9]

"The prisoners were assembled in a room at 12 o'clock," reported the Richmond *Daily Dispatch,* "and after being formed in a hollow square around a table, were informed of the order of General Winder."[10]

Captain Turner had prepared folded slips of paper bearing the names of the other seventy-four Union captains incarcerated at Libby. He spread those slips out across the table and urged the men to select one among themselves to make the fatal drawing of two names. After some talk, Capt. Henry Washington Sawyer, Co. K, 1st New Jersey Cavalry, countered the proposal by suggesting that Rev. Joseph T. Brown, 6th Maryland Cavalry, draw the names.

Reluctantly, Brown agreed. As the others watched in complete silence, he hesitantly drew the first slip of paper off the top of the table and handed it to Captain Turner. Slowly and methodically he drew the second and handed it over to Turner as well.

When Turner opened the folded slips of paper he saw the names Henry W. Sawyer and John M. Flinn of Company F, 51st Indiana Infantry.

"When the names were read out," reported the *Daily Dispatch,* "Sawyer heard it with no apparent emotion, remarking that someone had to be drawn and he could stand it as well as anyone else." But, according to the newspaper, Flinn became "white and very depressed" and later fainted.[11]

Sawyer, aged thirty-three, remained stoic throughout the afternoon. Formerly a carpenter in Cape May, New Jersey, before the war, he had quickly enlisted on April 15, 1861, at Trenton, when the hostilities first began. He had served bravely since then and had only been captured the previous month after being wounded in the thigh and cheek during the Battle of Brandy Station, Virginia, on June 9. After being treated at a hospital established at Culpeper Court House he had been transferred to Richmond's Libby Prison, arriving on June 15.

The two hostages were informed their execution would be in ten days. When told they had permission to write their next of kin, Flinn only requested to speak with a priest, further indicating he had no one to whom he wished to write. Sawyer, on the other hand, immediately sat down to write his wife and family.

"I am under the necessity of informing you that my prospect looks very dark," he wrote. "This morning all the Captains now prisoners at the

A Harper's Weekly *sketch of Capt. Henry W. Sawyer, Co. K, 1st New Jersey Cavalry, a POW in Richmond chosen for execution by Confederate authorities in retaliation for the Union executions of Corbin and McGraw.*

Libby military prison drew lots for two to be executed. It fell to my lot. Myself and Capt. Flinn, of the Fifty first Indiana infantry, will be executed for two Captains executed by Gen. Burnside. The Provost-General, J. H. Winder, assures me that the Secretary of War of the Southern Confederacy will permit yourself and my children to visit me before I'm executed. . . . My situation is hard to be borne, and I cannot think of dying without seeing you and the children . . . I am resigned to whatever is in store for me, with the consolation that I die without having committed any crime. I have no trial, no jury, nor am I charged with any crime, but it fell to my lot."[12]

"Sawyer wrote a letter home," admitted the Richmond *Daily Dispatch* the following day, "and read it aloud [and] coming to the last part of it, saying, 'farewell, my dear wife, farewell my dear children, farewell, mother,' he begged those standing by to excuse him, and turning aside, burst into tears."[13]

Once that letter was received by Sawyer's wife, it was published in newspapers throughout the North. Similar to the outrage expressed in Southern newspapers with the news of Corbin's and McGraw's executions, the Northern newspapers became incensed over Sawyer's and Flinn's plight. Within days, Confederate and Union papers were sparring back and forth with heated editorials.

*John M. Flinn, Co. F, 51st
Indiana Infantry, also chosen by
Confederate authorities in retalia-
tion for the Corbin-McGraw
execution as he was depicted in*
Harper's Weekly.

"When [his impending execution] became known to Capt. Sawyer's friends in Philadelphia," reported the *Philadelphia Press,* "they induced our respected townsman, Capt. Wilmon Whilden, long associated with the steamboat interest in this city, to visit Washington to ascertain the policy of the Government in regard to the inhuman threat. . . . He was kindly received by the President and the Secretary of War, and carried back to Philadelphia, from them, the assurance that the Government will adopt such a course as would possibly prevent the execution of Capts. Sawyer and Flinn, and at all events punish it fearlessly and promptly."[14]

Actually Whilden had accompanied Mrs. Sawyer on the July 14 trip to Washington and had met with New Jersey congressman J. T. Nixon. It was Nixon who had arranged the meeting with Lincoln and Stanton. After reviewing the case and Mrs. Sawyer's letter, Lincoln and Stanton advised the couple to return the following day while they tried to develop some plan of action to prevent the execution. Throughout that afternoon the president, vice president, secretary of war, and several other cabinet members and advisers continued to discuss the matter. That evening a member of the group finally realized that they had a "trump card" lying in a bed at Chesapeake Hospital near Fortress Monroe!

Back on June 26 Col. Samuel P. Spear and his 11th Pennsylvania Cavalry along with about 200 men, mounted, of different regiments, under Lt. Col. Hasbrouck Davis of the 12th Illinois Cavalry, were operating in the area of Hanover County, Virginia, as part of Maj. Gen. John A. Dix's Peninsula campaign, assigned to destroy the Virginia Central Railroad bridge over the South Anna River. After successfully completing that task and also destroying the Confederate quartermaster's depot at Hanover Station, Colonel Spear and his staff happened to notice in an article in a Richmond newspaper that Confederate general Robert E. Lee's second son, Brig. Gen. William H. F. "Rooney" Lee, had been wounded in the thigh by a pistol ball at the battle of Brandy Station on June 9 and had been taken to "Hickory Hill," a family friend's country estate in Hanover County, Virginia, owned by William F. Wickham. Spear also learned from the article that Lee was still there being nursed back to health by his mother, Mary, and his two sisters, Mildred and Agnes. Realizing "Hickory Hill" was just a short distance from where they were, Spear's regiment rode down upon the estate and captured Rooney Lee without resistance.[15]

"Colonel Spear's conduct has been gallant and judicious," Dix reported to his superiors on June 28. "General W. H. F. Lee was found at his house, not recovered from his wound, but was placed in an easy carriage and brought in. I had him examined this morning by my medical director, and, on the report of the latter, have directed him to be sent to the Chesapeake Hospital . . . [h]e had a flesh wound in the thigh, the ball having passed entirely through it."[16]

"His retention settles all questions about [the execution of] our officers" declared Lieutenant Colonel Ludlow, when the importance of the captive was realized. But although they knew they could trump the South with this highly important POW, Lincoln, Stanton, and the others spent the remainder of the evening discussing the agonizing decision of whether they would actually follow through if worse came to worse. All of those present fully realized how volatile retaliation on a POW of Rooney Lee's stature and name would be.[17]

Whilden and Mrs. Sawyer returned to the White House the following morning of July 15 and were told government officials had been up until 3:00 a.m. discussing the case. They were assured the government had developed a plan and all that could be done would be. Afterwards, Whilden and Mrs. Sawyer proceeded on to City Point, Virginia, on a flag-of-truce boat in an attempt to visit her husband before returning home.[18]

"The President directs that you immediately place General W. H. F. Lee and another officer selected by you not below the rank of captain, prisoner of war, in close confinement and under strong guard," Gen. Henry W. Halleck ordered Colonel Ludlow as soon as Mrs. Sawyer and Whilden had left the city, "and that you notify Mr. R. Ould, Confederate agent for exchange of prisoners of war, that if Capt. H. W. Sawyer, [1st] New Jersey Volunteer Cavalry, and Capt. John M. Flinn, [51st] Indiana Volunteers, or any other officers or men in the service of the United States . . . be executed by the enemy, the aforementioned prisoners will be immediately hung in retaliation. It is also directed that immediately on receiving official or other authentic information of the execution of Captain Sawyer and Captain Flinn, you will proceed to hang General Lee and the other rebel officer . . . and that you notify Robert Ould, esq., of said proceeding and assure him that the Government of the United States will proceed to retaliate for every similar barbarous violation of the laws of civilized war."[19]

"[T]he Confederate Government will not be intimidated by such threats," declared the Richmond *Daily Dispatch* once the Union threat became public. "The people call for the death of these two Yankees and it is useless to delay. . . . It is hoped that the Executive will see fit to give the order for execution immediately; and as we now have over 500 Federal Officers in our hands, besides 5,000 and 6,000 privates, it is in the power of the Government to carry retaliation to a very bitter extreme."[20]

Confederate officials, however, saw the situation quite differently.

"[I]n the lone hours of the night I groan in sorrow at his captivity," admitted a worried Gen. Robert E. Lee about his son in a letter to the family after the Federal announcement. "But we must bear it, exercise all our patience, and do nothing to aggravate the evil. This, besides injuring ourselves, would [only] rejoice our enemies."[21]

"I have . . . refrained from the exercise of such retaliation," President Davis complained again to President Lincoln, "because of its obvious tendency to lead to war of indiscriminate massacre on both sides."[22]

"The action on the part of our government plunged the Confederate authorities into a dilemma," observed one Union officer being confined at Libby Prison.

The influential leaders . . . demanded that proceedings
should be suspended in the blood-curdling drama about
to be opened with the death of Sawyer and Flinn. On the
other hand, some of the rank and file of the Confederacy,
crazed with hate for northern men and northern senti-
ment, were demanding their death, and the selection of
other hostages . . . [for] an era of terrible retaliation the
end of which no one could foretell.[23]

As newspaper editors in the North and the South got into the fray,
Confederate officials allowed July 16 to pass without incident. No announcement was made one way or the other but Union officials later
learned that Sawyer's and Flinn's executions had been postponed without
any new date being set. Union authorities also learned that when Mrs.
Sawyer and her escort had arrived at City Point, they were brusquely denied entry into the Confederate States.

"Mrs. Sawyer and Mr. W. Whilden cannot be permitted to land at
City Point," Robert Ould chastised in a dispatch to Union authorities
when they complained about the incident. "I am sorry they have been put
to the trouble of coming. I have certainly at no time hinted that they
would be permitted to land. If any person has stated to them that they
could, it has been done without proper authority."[24]

As the controversy continued, Lincoln, Stanton, and Ludlow agonized
over what to do next. The publicity was reaching overwhelming proportions while public opinion was being fanned by the newspapers to a
fevered pitch. "No amount of savagery on the part of the rebels should
compel us to adopt the habits of savages," the New York Times insisted.
"We certainly recommend it to our men not to surrender," declared the
Richmond Daily Enquirer, "[and if] our words could, by any means, reach
the Yankee soldiers, we would also tell them that their fate, if they come
here as prisoners, cannot be a very bright one."[25]

The controversy deepened when Union officials announced that the
second officer chosen as a hostage for retaliation was Captain Winder, son
of John H. Winder, the Confederate commissary general of prisoners, who
was currently incarcerated at the Carroll Prison annex of Old Capitol
Prison in Washington, D.C.

"Yesterday afternoon the rebel Gen. Fitzhugh Lee and Capt. Winder
were removed from the McClellan Hospital to Fortress Monroe and placed

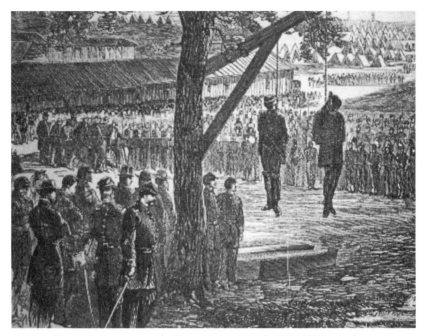

A typical military execution by hanging during the Civil War as shown in Harper's Weekly.

in a casemate, under guard," reported the *New York Times* of July 19, "and notice was sent to the rebel Government that if they executed Capts. Sawyer and Flinn . . . Gen. Lee and Capt. Winder will be executed in retaliation."[26]

"As Jefferson Davis does by Sawyer and Flinn," a New Jersey newspaper proudly proclaimed in its editorial, "so shall we do by Lee and Winder."[27]

Similar sentiments were expressed in editorials throughout the North while high-ranking Union officials were ecstatic with the prospect of having such highly political hostages in their possession. "I am satisfied," declared an excited Colonel Ludlow, "that Sawyer and Flinn will not be executed. [This matter is now] settled by the prompt and significant selections of Lee and Winder."[28]

"[O]ur authorities selected General Fitzhugh Lee and Captain Winder," agreed a Union official, "rightly surmising that the influential connection of those two officers in the Confederacy would prevent the threatened execution of the Union captains."[29]

Gen. W. H. F. "Rooney" Lee, son of Confederate general Robert E. Lee, captured on June 26, 1863, and held as a hostage, chosen for execution by Union authorities if the Confederate government proceeded with the Sawyer-Flinn executions.
LIBRARY OF CONGRESS

Curiously, though, Confederate authorities displayed little reaction to this second announcement. For one thing General Winder had checked and verified the location of his son, Capt. William Sidney Winder, and all other relatives they had in the Confederate service. None had been captured. In fact, no one named Winder could be found on any of the POW rolls previously turned over to Colonel Ould by Union authorities.

Ludlow, Hoffman, Stanton, and Lincoln continued to relish their good fortune for nearly three months until they received a letter from a Capt. Robert H. Tyler, 8th Virginia Infantry, a Confederate soldier incarcerated in Old Capitol Prison.

"On the 16th of July," Tyler complained, "I was taken from our Confederate officers in the Old Capitol and placed in close confinement, as [Prison] Superintendent [William P.] Wood supposed, as a hostage for Captains Sawyer and Flinn. . . . I was placed in close confinement the same day that General Lee and Captain Winder were, and it was believed by all the officers of the prison that I was a hostage for Sawyer and Flinn . . . I am extremely anxious to know why I am held. Superintendent Wood has tried in vain to find out."[30]

Immediately, Tyler's letter caused Union officials to scramble for an explanation.

Brig. Gen. Samuel P. Spear, 11th Pennsylvania Cavalry, who assisted in the capture of Gen. W. H. F. Lee, which brought the "officially sanctioned" retaliation executions to a halt. ROGER HUNT COLLECTION AT USAMHI

"I have just received your telegram of the 6th instant, inquiring where Captain Winder, hostage for Captain Sawyer, is confined," declared Ludlow in a quickly issued dispatch to Col. William Hoffman on October 7. "I do not know. When I received the order from Major-General Halleck to select General Lee and another officer not below the rank of Captain, there was none of the latter grade in confinement within the Department of Virginia. In acknowledging the receipt of the order, I so stated. I was informed afterward that Captain Winder had been selected. I supposed that he was in confinement with other Confederate officers under your direction."[31]

"Captain Tyler is in error in his reference to Captain Winder as having been held as a hostage," Hoffman reluctantly, but finally, admitted on November 9. "We hold no prisoners of war by the name and rank referred to. Captain Tyler, instead of Winder, was placed in close confinement at the Old Capitol by order of the General-in-Chief [Halleck] when General Lee was likewise so confined at Fort Monroe."[32]

Exactly who was responsible for the confusion in names, who released such information to the press, or how the confusion actually began is unclear. Ludlow was ordered to confine Lee and another officer on July 15. According to official records, Hoffman was indeed notified of Captain Tyler's selection as a hostage in this situation on July 16 while the first newspaper account about Lee and Winder's confinement as hostages appeared in the *New York Times* on July 19. So the confusion began sometime during that three-day period of July 16 to July 19. Why Hoffman allowed the references to a Captain Winder to continue for so long cannot be determined. The possibility of them using it as a form of public propaganda fails to explain why Union authorities privately, behind the scenes, continued to refer to the incarceration in confidential official correspondence. By all appearances, the officials involved in those communications sincerely believed Winder's son was in custody. Perhaps Hoffman simply failed to make the connection between the selection of this hostage and the Lee situation. After all, he was notified of Tyler being selected by Col. John C. Kelton, who was acting under orders of General Halleck, and apparently neither man made official notification to Ludlow. Or perhaps the root of all the confusion grew out of the capture of Lt. Robert W. Brown, aide-de-camp to Gen. John H. Winder, during Dix's Peninsula campaign. Several reports of his apprehension, merely mentioning that "Gen. Winder's aide was taken prisoner" circulated among Union commanders during that second week of May. Whatever the case, Ludlow was soon afterwards relieved from duty as agent for prisoner exchange and replaced by Brig. Gen. Sullivan A. Meredith.[33]

The politics of retaliation slowly ground to a halt as government officials on both sides became more cooperative in working out some kind of a peaceful solution. All executions and threats of them were temporarily suspended as the talks continued.

"Since our action in the cases of Corbin and McGraw," Robert Ould proudly reminded the Confederate secretary of war, James A. Seddon, "the Yankees have not executed any of our officers or men for recruiting within their (so-called) lines."[34]

Sawyer and Flinn, who had been isolated in individual cellar rooms beneath Libby Prison, were removed by the Confederate authorities sometime around the first week of October and returned to the general prison population on the upper floors without fanfare. Once this became known to Union officials, Lee and Tyler were in turn removed from their isolation and placed among their fellow prisoners. Within a few weeks, both were transferred to Fort Lafayette Prison in New York harbor.

"I see by the papers that our son has been sent to Fort Lafayette," Gen. Robert E. Lee remarked in a letter to his wife dated November 21, 1863.

"Any place would be better than Fort Monroe, with [Maj. Gen. Benjamin F.] Butler in command, [but] his long confinement is very grievous to me."[35]

During the following December, Rooney Lee received word that his wife, Charlotte, was ill and near death. He and other relatives made an application to Union authorities to be allowed a forty-eight hour pass to be with her. Rooney's brother, Custis Lee, of equal rank as Rooney, formally volunteered in writing to take his place as a hostage until Rooney could return to the prison but all requests were denied. Charlotte died on December 26.[36]

Although, officially, all prisoner exchanges had been suspended due to the previous collapse of all formal agreements between the two governments, during the next several weeks negotiations quietly began to exchange Lee.

"I have reason to believe that if the government will propose to exchange General Lee for myself, the only Federal general here," wrote Neal Dow, being held at Libby, after being encouraged by Confederate officials to write, "the proposition will be favorably entertained and the exchange effected."[37]

"It has been intimated from Richmond," advised Ethan A. Hitchcock, the Union's new commissioner of prisoner exchange assigned in December of 1863, "that if we will consent to exchange General Lee and two officers of the grade of captain the rebel authorities will give us [Brigadier] General [Neal] Dow [captured at Port Hudson, Louisiana, June 30, 1863] and Captains Sawyer and Flinn."[38]

"I am directed by the Secretary of War to say that in making the exchange," Hoffman cautioned, "you will please bear in mind that it is authorized only with the understanding that both Captains Flinn and Sawyer are to be exchanged; without this, the exchange will not be made."[39]

Gen. Neal Dow's son and a family friend, Charles A. Stackpole of Portland, Maine, immediately went to Washington to meet with Maine senators Lot M. Morrill and William P. Fessenden and Vice Pres. Hannibal Hamlin, formerly of Maine, to work out the necessary steps for a possible exchange.

"General Lee was the most influentially connected of any Confederate officer then in the hands of the North," admitted Neal Dow, "while I was the only northern officer of equal rank held by the South. His friends on the one side, and mine on the other, had been most active in bringing about the proposition for the exchange."[40]

As both sides continued to covertly negotiate, no information was released to the press or to any of the prisoners involved. Eventually, however, negotiations between the two sides were leaked.

"Brig. Gen. W. H. F. Lee has just been informed by letter, from a gentleman direct from Washington, that a proposition has been made by the Confederate authorities to exchange Brig. Gen. Neal Dow and Captains Sawyer and Flinn for himself and any two captains whom the United States Government might designate," Capt. Robert Tyler wrote in a letter to Col. William Hoffman dated February 20, 1864. "It was also stated in this letter that the United States Government had acceded to the proposition and that orders had been issued to have the exchange carried out. As I have been held as one of the hostages for captains Sawyer and Flinn, I would respectfully request that I may be selected as one of the captains for exchange."[41]

Hoffman agreed that Tyler should be one of the officers exchanged and on February 25 had him and William Henry Fitzhugh Lee transferred back to Fortress Monroe to await a flag-of-truce boat for conveyance down the James River to City Point for the transaction.

Finally, on March 14, 1864, Sawyer, Flinn, and Dow were told to pack up immediately for a trip to Fortress Monroe. They left Richmond's Libby Prison at 11:00 A.M. on a flag-of-truce boat and arrived at City Point at 7:30 that evening. There, as Lee and Tyler crossed over the gangplank into the Confederate boat, Sawyer, Flinn, and Dow crossed the gangplank onto the *New York* and headed to freedom at Fortress Monroe.[42]

Although some unsanctioned retaliation executions occurred in the field between individual commanders after this incident, both governments officially abandoned the practice after the Sawyer-Flinn and Lee controversy. Within three months, however, officials of both sides had developed an entirely new concept of retaliation that would utilize large groups of POWs.

Chapter 8

Prisoners as Pawns

CHARLESTON AND MORRIS ISLAND

The year 1863 is often referred to as the turning point of the war. Battles of that year, such as Chancellorsville, Brandy Station, Gettysburg, the fall of Vicksburg, and Chickamauga, are all considered decisive engagements that eventually took their toll on the Confederacy. In addition to Lincoln's Emancipation Proclamation and the death of "Stonewall" Jackson, 1863 brought the rise of Gen. Ulysses S. Grant. The year was also the most decisive juncture for its prisoners of war. The exchange cartel, or agreement between the Union and Confederacy for exchanging POWs, collapsed that year. Exchanges halted, prison populations dramatically increased, the number and sizes of military prisons greatly expanded, and conditions within the facilities drastically deteriorated.

It was also in that year that acts of retaliation between the two governments climaxed, going way beyond man for man recrimination to eventually using entire groups of prisoners as pawns. And that retalitory policy seems to have developed exactly where the war had begun—in Charleston Harbor.

On July 10, 1863, Union troops stormed onto Morris Island to launch a long and bitter campaign to take control of Charleston Harbor. By August the city of Charleston, South Carolina, was under siege. "The Federal batteries on Morris Island," according to Charles M. Busbee of the 5th North Carolina Regiment, "were shelling the City of Charleston, imperiling the lives of non-combatants, consisting of women, children, and old men." The citizens of this community endured the siege for one full year before Confederate authorities finally made one bold desperate move to save the city.[1]

"The enemy continue their bombardment of the city with increased vigor," complained Confederate major general Samuel Jones, commander, Department of South Carolina, on June 1, 1864. "I can take care of a party of, say fifty Yankee prisoners," he told Gen. Braxton Bragg. "Can you not send me that number, including a general . . . to be confined in parts of the city still occupied by citizens, but under the enemy's fire?"[2]

Such a proposal wasn't an entirely new idea to Confederates stationed at Charleston. A similar suggestion had been made over a year earlier by Lt. Col. John L. Branch, commander of Charleston's Rifle Regiment and former commander of Fort Morris, within weeks of the island being taken by Union forces. "It has been suggested by my brother, Mr. D. W. Branch," he advised in a dispatch directed at Gen. Thomas Jordan, Confederate brigadier general P. G. T. Beauregard's chief of staff at Charleston, "that the difficulty of holding that portion of Morris Island now in the possession of the enemy (after we shall have retaken it) might be [held] by establishing a camp there for holding under heavy guard all Yankee prisoners, officers and privates, [to be exposed to the enemy's bombardment] until it can be strongly fortified."[3]

Nor was Branch's idea an entirely new concept to the art of warfare. "[T]he practice of exposing prisoners of war to the fire of the attacking force is as old as the fact that weak and wicked parties must fall under the blows of justice," one Union commander later complained.[4]

But back on July 18, 1863, Branch's original proposal was immediately turned down. "[I]t is not considered in accordance with the usages of war," he was told, "to use our prisoners as a means of defense or protection." Now, however, after a year of constant bombardment, the Confederate officials were apparently willing to reconsider. Jones's request was forwarded to the Confederate secretary of war who, in turn, presented it to Pres. Jefferson Davis.[5]

"General S. Jones, at Charleston, asks for fifty officers of rank, Federal prisoners, to be sent to him at Charleston for special use in Charleston during the siege," Adj. Samuel Cooper advised Gen. Howell Cobb, commandant of the Confederate military prison at Macon, Georgia, on June 9. "The President approves the application . . . send the number without delay to General Jones under a suitable guard."[6]

The POW facility at Macon confined only Union officers. General Cobb chose fifty among them for transport to South Carolina. The group, consisting of five generals and forty-five field officers, arrived in Charleston on Sunday, June 12.

"[B]rought hither to share the pleasures of the bombardment," reported the *Charleston Mercury.* "These prisoners we understand will be furnished with comfortable quarters in that portion of the city most exposed to the enemy's fire."[7]

This group of Union POWs, consisting of five brigadier generals, eleven colonels, twenty-five lieutenant colonels, and nine majors, were split into two groups of twenty-five. One group was taken to Charleston's Roper Hospital, near Calhoun and Courtenay streets on the west side of town, for confinement while the other was taken to the O'Connor House, owned by Col. James O'Connor, several blocks southeast of the hospital at 180 Broad Street. Both groups were apparently unaware they were being held as hostages under fire. They knew Charleston's other POW facilities, the City Jail Yard on the southeast part of town, the Guard House at Broad and Meeting Streets, and the Charleston Race Course on the northwest outskirts of town, were all filled beyond capacity. Since those places were so crowded and filthy, the officers merely assumed they were transferred to new quarters out of respect for their rank. The luxurious surroundings of the hospital and the opulent private residence were a welcome change from the small, crowded, plain clapboard barracks in which they had been confined at Macon.

Roper Hospital was a massive masonry structure with three stories of covered porches across the front. "[We] passed through the gateway of 'Roper' into the beautiful garden of the hospital," marveled one prisoner later held there. "On our right is a palmetto, on our left an orange tree, while around us bloom flowers of every hue."[8]

"Our surroundings at this place were as pleasant as we could expect," reported another prisoner. "The officials, too, were gentlemanly and courteous and seemed really desirous of making our condition as comfortable as was in their power."[9]

The prisoners were assigned quarters on the third floor *piazza.* "[T]he hard floor seeming a luxury," recalled another prisoner, "and the place itself a paradise."[10]

Those confined at the O'Connor house were just as pleased with their surroundings. The home was a huge, white, three-story clapboard structure having four large Greek Corinthian columns, two stories high, supporting a large porch roof across the front of the house. A large two-story addition was attached at the rear of the residence.

"Five generals and 45 field officers of the U.S. Army, all of them prisoners of war, have been sent to this city for safekeeping," Jones advised Maj. Gen. John G. Foster, the district's Union commander, the next morning. "[T]hey are provided with commodious quarters in a part of the city occupied by non-combatants, the majority of whom are women and children. It is proper, however, that I should inform you that it is a part of the city which has been for many months exposed day and night to the fire of your guns."[11]

"Many months [ago]," responded Foster,

> Major-General Gillmore, U.S. Army, notified General Beauregard, then commanding at Charleston, that the city would be bombarded. This notice was given [so] that . . . women and children be spared from harm . . . I must, however, protest against your action in thus placing defenseless prisoners of war in a position exposed to constant bombardment. It is an indefensible act of cruelty, . . . designed only to prevent the continuance of our fire upon Charleston . . . a depot for military supplies. It contains not merely arsenals but also [munitions] foundries and factories. . . . In its ship-yards several armed ironclads have already been completed, while others are still upon the stocks in course of construction. Its wharves and the banks of the rivers on both sides of the city are lined with batteries. To destroy [military sites] is therefore our object and duty. You seek to defeat this effort . . . by placing unarmed and helpless prisoners under our fire.

"[T]he manner in which the fire has been directed from the commencement shows beyond doubt that its object was the destruction of the city itself, and every part of it, and not, as you assume, to destroy certain military and naval works in and immediately around it," Jones angrily replied.

The shells have been thrown at random, at any and all hours, day and night, falling promiscuously in the heart of the city, at points remote from each other and from the works you mention. . . . [T]hey have not fallen in or been concentrated for any time upon any particular locality . . . but they have searched the city in every direction, indicating no purpose . . . of accomplishing any military result, but rather the design of destroying private property and killing some persons, no matter whom.[13]

Immediately after responding to Jones's original dispatch, Foster had notified officials in Washington of the Confederate move and added, "I respectfully ask that an equal number of rebel officers of equal rank may be sent to me, in order that I may place them under the enemy's fire as long as our officers are exposed in Charleston."[14]

Later Foster confided to the chief of staff, Maj. Gen. Henry W. Halleck, "I think the cruel determination of the rebels to place our officers in Charleston under our fire is an evidence of their vindictive weakness and of the destruction that the city is sustaining from our fire. I hope the President will decide to retaliate in the manner proposed."[15]

Within days Halleck responded. "The Secretary of War has directed an equal number of rebel generals and field-officers be sent to you . . . to be treated in precisely the same manner as the enemy treat ours—that is, to be placed in positions where they will be most exposed to the fire of the rebels."[16]

Back when Foster had originally received Jones's notification, one Union commander advised to continue "the usual fire on the city, with a constant change of direction, to avoid, if possible, the design of the enemy to bring their prisoners under our fire." The officer then offered the opinion, "the fact of the enemy's being so anxious for an immediate reply, I am led to believe the whole thing a ruse, or at least only a threat not yet carried out."[17]

The truth was, the hostages at the hospital were slightly beyond the northwest range of the Union's Morris Island batteries while those at the O'Connor house, unbeknownst to the hostages themselves, were in more danger, well within reach of it, being in the "heart" of the city as Jones had referred. In fact, all of the city below Calhoun Street was within easy range of the Federal guns and received the most extensive damage. It was in the O'Connor house that Jones had placed the five highest-ranking prisoners.

Still, neither location sustained any severe damage from the heavy shells being pumped into the city, although several buildings near the O'Connor house were eventually reduced to rubble, and shrapnel from nearby exploding shells occasionally hit the hospital. In the meantime, Union officials continually interrogated any Confederate deserters leaving the city or debriefed any escaping POWs in an attempt to find out exactly where the hostages were being kept.[18]

For the Union's retaliation the Lincoln administration decided to use POWs from their Fort Delaware Prison facility. Stanton directed Col. William Hoffman, commissary general of prisoners, to make the arrangements and he, in turn, notified Brig. Gen. Albin F. Schoepf, the prison commandant, to make the selection. All the men chosen showed little or no reaction to the event.

"[O]ur chief reason for regarding the matter with little or no apprehension," recalled Confederate brigadier general Basil Duke, one of the hostages to be sent from Fort Delaware, "was the fact that none of us believed the truth of the report that the Federal prisoners had been placed under fire. We, therefore, had no fear that we ourselves would be subjected to any such ordeal."[19]

Once the fifty were chosen they were sent by steamer to Hilton Head, South Carolina, and turned over to Major General Foster. They arrived June 30, whereupon Foster immediately notified Jones the following day.

"I would respectfully request information as to what portion of the city [your hostages] are confined," Foster slyly inquired. "[In]form me of the degree of exposure to which they are subjected; whether in the part of the city most, or in that least, exposed, or that exposed in a medium degree . . . that I may treat in the same manner a like number of your officers of equal rank that are now placed in my hands by the Government."[20]

Once Foster's message was delivered, Confederate authorities encouraged their Union officers to write a letter in response. "The journals of this morning inform us, for the first time, that 5 general officers of the Confederate service have arrived at Hilton Head," the five Union generals being held at the O'Connor house wrote in a letter addressed to Foster the next day,

> with a view to their being subjected to the same treatment that we are receiving here. We think it is just to ask for these officers every kindness and courtesy that you can

extend to them, in acknowledgment of the fact that we, at this time, are as pleasantly and comfortably situated as is possible for prisoners of war, receiving from the Confederate authorities every privilege that we could desire or expect, nor are we unnecessarily exposed to fire.[21]

To their letter Major General Jones attached a recommendation that all of the prisoners be exchanged with those in Foster's custody, hoping it could be arranged between the two even though their respective governments had previously ceased all official exchanges of commissioned officers.

"I fully reciprocate your desire for an exchange of prisoners," Foster responded on July 4, "but before any steps can be taken to effect it, it will be necessary for you to withdraw from exposure to our fire those officers now confined in Charleston." Foster then added, "I have not yet placed [my] prisoners in a similar position of exposure."[23]

While Foster contacted Union authorities about Jones' proposal and was given the go ahead, Jones responded to this last dispatch by reemphasizing that although he could not reveal the exact locations of his prisoners they were "pleasantly and comfortably situated" and not "unnecessarily exposed to fire," adding his

regret that you should require as a condition . . . that I should remove from their present location the U.S. prisoners of war now in this city. Such a course on my part would be an implied admission that those officers are unduly exposed and treated with unnecessary rigor, which they have themselves assured you in their letter . . . is not the case . . . [and] to require a change of location which you have every reason to know the prisoners do not themselves desire is to throw an unnecessary obstacle in the way.

Jones then closed with: "The change I most prefer would be to send them to your headquarters."[23]

Another week passed before Foster could advise Jones that the Union secretary of war had granted permission, "being a special one," for the exchange of the fifty prisoners that they each held. On August 3, 1864, as the uninterrupted bombardment of the city continued, the exchange of the hostages took place. At about the same time, Jones was notified by Confederate authorities that, as a result of Union general George Stoneman's raids in the vicinity of Macon and Andersonville, and the fear that his forces might attempt to release the POWs at the various Confederate prisons in their path, it would be necessary to send a large contingency of prisoners to Charleston for confinement while others were being sent to Savannah.

Jones wanted no more prisoners. His Charleston facilities were still filled to capacity and the recent situation ending in the exchange had developed too much controversy. "Please have the order revoked," he pleaded in a dispatch to Confederate secretary of war James A. Seddon. "It is exceedingly embarrassing to me to have so many prisoners to provide for."[24]

In the following days Jones continued making requests to have the order rescinded but was repeatedly told there was no alternative. As the prisoners began to arrive, Jones distributed them throughout the city. Nearly a hundred were confined in the Guard House, several hundred in the City Jail, the wall-enclosed jail yard, and the City Workhouse next door, and several hundred more were confined at the Race Course. Eventually several hundred were accepted from Andersonville and 600 from Macon. Because of severe overcrowding at the city jail and the workhouse, 86 of the officers were moved a few days later to Roper Hospital and 30 were placed in the O'Connor house. "Please have U.S. officers, prisoners of war, now here removed to some other place," Jones again begged his superiors. "It is very inconvenient and unsafe to keep them here."[25]

When Foster learned that more Federal POWs had arrived in Charleston he naturally assumed Jones intended again to use human shields to protect the city. His suspicions seemed to be supported when he learned that some of the officers were moved to the hospital and the O'Connor house. Almost immediately, Foster requested of Major General Halleck that 600 "rebel officers" of various grades to be sent to him for confinement near Union positions for retaliation.

"The Secretary of War has directed that 600 rebel officers, prisoners of war, be sent to you, to be confined, exposed to fire, and treated in the same manner as our officers," Halleck responded a few days later. "No exchanges will be made without special instructions of the War Department. Any offer for exchange will be communicated here for the action of the Secretary of War."[26]

During the next several days Colonel Hoffman and General Schoepf went over the Fort Delaware prison rolls very slowly and methodically. From those lists they chose 186 prisoners from Virginia, 111 from North Carolina, 60 from Georgia, 49 from Tennessee, 35 from Kentucky, 31 from Louisiana, 27 from Arkansas, 26 from Alabama, 24 from South Carolina, 22 from Mississippi, 10 from Florida, 8 from Missouri, 6 from Maryland, and 5 from Texas, representing all of the states having regiments in the Confederate service. The names of these officers were then announced to the prisoners on Saturday morning, August 13.

"At an early hour the Sergeant came in and announced that the names of such persons as were to be sent off would soon be called, in the yard," recalled one prisoner.

> [S]oon Gen. Schoepf, Capt. [George W.] Ahl, and sundry
> clerks, with sergeants and guards, made their appearance
> . . . Calls were made first for field officers; and then for
> captains and lieutenants, running down the rolls in an ir-
> regular manner . . . upon what principle the elections
> were made, it was impossible to tell.[27]

"When the M's were called on the roll I could hardly contain myself," recalled prisoner John Ogden Murray, captain, 11th Virginia Cavalry. "[W]hen my name was called I could have shouted for joy; and I really felt sorry that all my comrades were not included in the list."[28]

"It was only a few weeks since [the previous] fifty Field Officers went away under a similar threat; and they had been duly exchanged," explained prisoner Walter G. MacRae, captain, Co. G, 7th North Carolina.

> We were so certain that this [too] was a bluff that every-
> one was anxious to go. Many, whose names were not on
> the list, gathered up their poor belongings—watches,
> rings, a little money—anything and everything of value
> which had escaped confiscation, and came and laid them
> down at the feet of [those who had been chosen] if haply
> they might persuade some one to exchange places."[29]

"Several officers [did] purchase their exchange," recalled prisoner Isaac Handy. "One—Lt. [Edmund] Mastin, of Alabama—gave a gold watch, which cost three hundred dollars in coin before the war. Two other gentlemen gave watches of less value."[30]

"In [another] case as much as $250 was paid for the privilege," recalled prisoner Abram Fulkerson, colonel, 63rd Tennessee Regiment.

> The officers purchasing these supposed privileges, assumed and answered to the names of their vendors when the final roll was called on leaving the prison, and while quite a number of these exchanges were made, none of them were detected by the Federal officers in charge.[31]

Back in South Carolina, on August 15, Major General Foster formally notified Maj. Gen. Sam Jones of his intentions:

> I have received information from deserters and also from prisoners of war that were exchanged for your prisoners on the 3rd instant, that a large number of officers of the U.S. Army, reported at about 600, are exposed to our fire in Charleston. I am surprised at this repeated violation of the usages of humane and civilized warfare, as I had hoped that the exchange of our prisoners formerly exposed would have ended the cruel treatment on your part. I . . . therefore, again protest against it and inform you that unless the prisoners are removed from Charleston and from under our fire an equal number of your prisoners of war now in our hands will be exposed to your fire.[32]

Jones denied that he had intentionally placed any POWs under Union fire and further maintained that the Macon and Andersonville prisoners were only in the city temporarily until a better location for their confinement could be established. He then offered to exchange prisoners with Foster, man for man and rank for rank, at any time.[33]

Foster ignored the exchange offer and continued his sanctimonious condemnation of the Confederate authorities in the city over the next several days. On August 18, he mentioned the exchange offer to his superiors in Washington. "The truth is," Foster privately confided with Halleck,

> they are so short of men as guards that they have no place to put their prisoners in except Charleston and Savannah. . . . As far as injury to them goes there can be none, for I know their exact position and direct the shells accordingly. As soon as the rebel officers arrive I shall place them immediately on Morris Island between [batteries] Wagner and Gregg.[34]

A week passed before an old side-wheel steamer, the *Crescent City*, arrived at the Fort Delaware wharf to transport the prisoners south. "At three o'clock p.m., August 20, the order came 'Fall into line all you men whose names shall be called and be ready for exchange'," recalled prisoner Murray.[35]

"The 600 passed out of the gate of the prison pen and were formed in two ranks on the outside," recalled another prisoner. "Ranks were opened, and what luggage the officers had and their clothing were thoroughly searched as a measure of precaution . . . [t]he inspection being complete, we were marched to the wharf, where we found the steamer."[36]

"When the head of the column passed the gangway . . .," explained prisoner Faulkerson,

> the guards directed us to pass down a ladder leading from the hatchway into the hold of the vessel. . . . [T]his hold, or hole, was below the water-line, without light, and very imperfectly ventilated from above. Lines of shelves about two feet wide, projecting from the walls of the vessel, from the bottom to the floor above, and running around the entire space allotted to us, one above the other, at a distance hardly sufficient to allow a man lying down to turn over, served as our berths or bunks, which were occupied by the officers lying head to foot.[37]

"The bunks did not afford sufficient room for all the prisoners," complained Capt. William H. Morgan, 11th Virginia Infantry, "consequently a good many lay on the floor of the deck between the bunks."[38]

The slow trip on the *Crescent City,* a large ocean steamer that routinely plied the water between New Orleans and Galveston before the war, was a harrowing experience in itself.

"About three-fourths of us became very sick shortly after leaving Fort Delaware," advised one prisoner.

> And as closely confined as we were, the spectacle was horrid—the entire floor covered with sick men—horribly sick, vomiting to a fearful extent by the disease, and groaning in a terrific manner—presented a sight too sickening to behold, and too repulsive to endure, and too wretched to describe. Even those of us who were not infected by the sickening malady, were made faint by the loathsome spectacle we were obliged to witness.[39]

"In two instances the guard placed in with us fainted," claimed another prisoner. "I heard one of them remark: 'A dog couldn't stand this.'"[40]

For security reasons only one hatch of the ship was left open, making the hold fairly dark and stifling hot, in addition to being crowded. A lack of rations and decent drinking water added to their misery. A battalion of infantry patrolled the deck and guarded the open hatch. Prisoners soon found conditions from the extreme August heat and poor ventilation of the hold unbearable. As many continued to suffer from seasickness, the filth and stench in the hold worsened while a lack of latrines and the refusal to allow captives on deck added vomit and excrement to the increasingly intolerable conditions.

Two gunboats, the *Dictator* and *Eutaw,* remained alongside the ship as an escort, while the naval supply steamer *Admiral* brought up the rear. Along the route the convoy stopped over at Fortress Monroe, Virginia, for a day or two, leaving the POWs confined in the hold. When they became rebellious about conditions, the prisoners were pacified for a time by being told they would be exchanged. When the convoy later resumed its southbound journey, they were then told the exchange would take place in Charleston.

Several days out, as the steamer neared Cape Romain, South Carolina, William Baxter, the second mate left in charge of the vessel during the night while the ship's captain, Daniel D. Latham, and first mate, John M. Brown, were down in their berths sleeping, noticed that the two gunboats had drifted back out of sight. Baxter steered the *Crescent City* toward shore, apparently, it was later alleged, with the intent to allow the POWs to escape.

"[M]any of . . . crew," advised prisoner Abram Fulkerson, "were with the vessel [from before the war]. They were sympathizers with the South, and when they could escape the vigilance of the guards and sentinels, they would extend the prisoners such little favors as they were able."[41]

"Great confusion at once ensued among the prisoners and also among the Federal officers," recalled one POW on board as the craft ran aground in shallow water near the shore.

> We . . . determined to . . . demand . . . the surrender of the vessel. It was a desperate under-taking, as it would have been almost certain destruction if we had attempted to reach the deck under the concentrated fire of one hundred muskets. Still, we . . . placed in the lead Van H. Manning, the brave and dashing Colonel of the Third Arkansas Infantry. Through him we made the demand upon the captain for surrender, and, to the surprise of some of us, he agreed to surrender the vessel.[42]

Captain Latham agreed on the condition that the officers, crew, and the guard units be exchanged at Charleston. When the crew of the *Admiral* had noticed the steamer making toward shore, they had lit lights and sent up rockets. According to Capt. James H. Prentiss, commanding the 157th Ohio Militia guard unit, Baxter had ignored the lights and rockets and continued in a direct line toward the Cape Romain lighthouse. In the confusion of the ship running aground, prisoner George W. Woolfolk escaped. Others started but were held back by the sentry. A standoff ensued as one of the gunboats, coming up from the rear, located the *Crescent City* and fired a warning shot as it steamed at full speed toward the stranded craft. The reappearance of the gunboats enabled the crew and guards to regain control of the vessel and the POWs were forced back down into the hold. Captain Latham and Second Mate Baxter were immediately arrested and placed in irons. Meanwhile, the escort craft remained at the side of the grounded vessel to guard against onshore Confederate attacks until high tide took the *Crescent City* back out into deeper water and the trip to Morris Island continued. "We were then driven in the middle deck or hold," complained one prisoner after the escape attempt, "the hatchways were closed [and] the port holes fastened so as to admit neither light nor air."[43]

"This was in August," added another prisoner,

> and the animal heat, which was greatly augmented by the heat from the smoke-stack, became so intolerable, and the smell of the place so offensive, that it was considered a great privilege to go to the water-closet for a few minutes, where one could get a breath of fresh air and enjoy the spray thrown upon one's body by the paddle-wheel. Of course every man remained there until he was driven out by the sentinel, regardless of the suffering and clamor of his comrades in the hold."[44]

The trip slowly continued along the coast, marked by numerous portages and several delays, including the court-martial of the ship's captain and second mate at Port Royal, and a brief stay at Hilton Head, where another prisoner escaped. The *Crescent City* finally steamed back up the coast and landed at Morris Island exactly eighteen days after leaving Fort Delaware—during the entire time the POWs being confined below deck. The prisoners, however, remained confined in the ship's hold for another two days while an onshore stockade pen was being completed.

"On 7 September, we disembarked at Morris Island," related prisoner Walter MacRae, "and when we finally came out into the light of day, and had a look at each other, we were astonished to note the ravages made by the terrible heat and the nauseous confinement. One could scarcely recognize his best friends."[45]

"We were ordered," added Murray, "to turn out and form in line on the beach. After forming and the counting of our number was finished the order was given to march. . . . We had not gone over [a] half-mile before some of our men, weakened from the eighteen days on the filthy prison ship, fell, from prostration, in the sand."[46]

The men were marched three miles along the beach to the stockade. Those who fell were ordered up at the point of a bayonet and force-marched to the pen by soldiers of the 54th Massachusetts Colored Regiment, who had been detailed to the Island as guards.

"[T]he stockade was erected on the beach about forty or fifty feet from the water," observed Busbee. "When we reached the stockade prison-pen-gate," advised Murray, "we were again halted, counted off by fours and sent inside the inclosure, where a negro sergeant assigned us to tents, putting four men in each small A-tent which would not comfortably hold more than two men."[47]

The stockade, consisting of about two acres, was square and built of twenty-foot pine logs buried upright in the sand at a depth of about five feet. These were cleated together with pine boards. A parapet for the guards ran along the top of the stockade to provide them a full view of the interior. About ten feet from the inside of the fence a rope, supported by stakes driven into the sand, served as the prison deadline. The tents were arranged in parallel rows, forming pathways between every two rows.

"At the head of the middle street," advised Murray, "was placed a Mitrailleuse Requa gun, loaded and ready to open upon our camp at a moment's notice."[48]

Morris Island is a four-mile-long expanse of sand, varying in width anywhere from a hundred yards at its narrowest point to half a mile wide at its broadest. Located four miles south of Charleston, it is separated from nearby James Island on the west by Vincent's Creek and a number of broad marshes intersected by numerous saltwater creeks. The Atlantic Ocean washes up along its eastern shore. Located at the entrance to the harbor, it had become a vital strategic location in the concentrated bombardment of Charleston. Along with its other siege guns, the Union had briefly erected an eight-inch, 200-pound Parrott rifle, dubbed the "Swamp Angel," in the marshes adjacent to Morris Island during the first weeks of August, and at 1:30 A.M. on August 22 the big gun was put into action, pumping out 150-pound incendiaries into the city at fifteen-minute intervals. The gun exploded after thirty-six rounds, so seacoast mortars, and later, a 30-pound Parrott rifle, were moved to the site to continue the assault.

The prison stockade had been built in front of what had been Battery Wagner, with the Star of the West Battery a little farther north down the beach toward the end of the Morris Island peninsula and Battery Gregg even farther down the beach at the point. "The stockade was about midway between Forts Wagner and Gregg," explained Fulkerson. "Our position," observed MacRae, "was such that every shot or shell from the guns on Sumter and Moultrie and other Confederate batteries, must either pass close over our head, or right through the pen."[49]

"The first night in the pen was not at all pleasant," complained prisoner Capt. Richard E. Frayser, C.S.A. Signal Corps, "firing commenced early that night, and fragments of Confederate shell thrown from Fort Moultrie fell in the pen."[50]

"The first evening and night the shelling was very heavy," prisoner Francis C. Barnes, 6th Virginia Infantry Regiment, agreed, "but none of us were killed. It seemed our guns got the range and fired over us."[51]

"Shells from the Confederate batteries were thrown with great precision into Fort Wagner," recalled Fulkerson, "passing immediately over our pen, and others exploded to our left and front."[52]

"[T]he stockade was placed in the line of fire of the Confederate batteries on Sullivan's Island which were shelling Battery Wagner," noted Busbee.

> The Confederate gunners would cut their fuses so as to endeavor to prevent any shell from exploding in our neighborhood, but on more than one occasion a shell exploded prematurely and on one occasion that I well remember, a shell burst directly over the stockade and threw several of its fragments among us.[53]

"This storm of shot and shell created some consternation upon the prisoners," one noted, "and at first caused something like a panic."[54]

During the first two days of their confinement in the stockade, the shelling activity remained somewhat subdued. Perhaps the gunners of both sides were simply testing and checking their range. After all, Federal gunners were well aware that Union officers were still distributed throughout the city—several locations of which they knew—and the Confederate artillerymen became aware of the Morris Island prisoners within hours of their confinement in the pen. "[T]he enemy is now landing Confederate officers, prisoners of war, on Morris Island," Confederate major general Jones immediately notified his superiors on August 7. "If the department thinks proper to retaliate by placing Yankee officers in Sumter and other batteries, let the order be given."[55]

No such order was given and the shelling continued sporadically until September 9. By then the gunners of both sides must have found their range and apparently believed they knew where all the prisoners were being held because on that day all hell broke loose in one of the most spectacular aerial displays any of these men, on either side, would ever witness.

"At early noon," reported one prisoner, "the Federal batteries on Morris Island, and all the guns of the Yankee fleet [around the harbor] opened on the Confederate forts and Charleston city."[56]

"They opened fire right over our heads," exclaimed a Confederate officer confined in the Morris Island stockade. "[Then] we saw a puff of smoke blow out from Fort Moultrie, and almost immediately, heard the rush of a fine, large shell. It passed howling over our heads and smashed into the nearest embrasure, where it exploded with much havoc."[57]

"It was a grand yet fearful sight to behold," marveled another prisoner.

> [E]very discharge . . . shook the sandy Island like the convulsive throes of an earthquake, and shook the entire frame from head to foot. Next was seen the fiery . . . element springing from the guns with the velocity of a shadow, and . . . soaring aloft into the smooth space above, a long fiery tail resembling that of a comet trailing behind. . . . When nearing the destined place, suddenly with the concussion of a thunderbolt it burst, and the fragments were heard singing the death knell on every side.[58]

"It was rather uncomfortable," reported Morris Island prisoner William Morgan,

> to . . . watch the big shells sailing through the air, which we could see at night by the fuse burning, and sometimes burst above us, instead of bursting in or above the Yankee forts 100 yards further on, and then listen at the fragments humming through the air and hear them strike the ground with a dull thud among the tents.[59]

"As it reached the zenith," a Union prisoner confined in Charleston described in witnessing one of the projectiles fired into the city from Morris Island,

> there came to our ears a prolonged, but not sharp,— 'Whish-ish-ish-ish-ish!' We watched it breathlessly, and it seemed to be long minutes . . .; then a thump upon the ground, and a vibration. . . . For a moment there was a dead silence. Then came a loud roar and the crash of breaking timber and crushing walls.[60]

"[F]or two or three hours the duel lasted," proclaimed Murray. "The shells from Sumter and our other batteries fell thick and fast upon the island, most of them uncomfortably close to our stockade."[61]

The shelling continued off and on for several weeks, but the dueling was never as intense as that which occurred on September 9. Eventually the POWs of both sides grew accustomed to the constant shelling above and around them. One Confederate prisoner confined on Morris Island later marveled: "One morning a large shell fell right at our feet and covered us all with sand, but fortunately did not explode." A Union prisoner confined in Charleston likewise recalled in amazement:

> One night a shell passed through a large building about a quarter of a mile from us. . . . The shell went through with a deafening crash. All was still for an instant; then it exploded with a dull roar followed by more crashing of timber and walls. The sound died away . . . succeeded by a moment of silence. Finally the great building fell, a shapeless heap of ruins. . . . This was the nearest to us that any shell came.[62]

Foster and Jones continued to bicker back and forth about using prisoners for retaliation. Finally, after six and a half weeks, both sides agreed to began moving their prisoners elsewhere. The Union officers held in the city of Charleston were moved farther inland to Florence and Columbia, South Carolina; the Confederate officers held on Morris Island were moved on October 21 to Fort Pulaski in Savannah, Georgia, for a time before eventually being returned to Fort Delaware for confinement. In all, only 558 of the original 600 removed from Fort Delaware were actually confined in the Morris Island stockade. Thirty-nine had been removed from the ship at Hilton Head Island and held in jail there before being transferred to Beaufort, South Carolina, and two prisoners escaped on the way to Morris Island while one died and was buried at sea.[63]

While confined within the stockade, three POWs died of disease and starvation, and two were shot and wounded by guards. Although several shells had burst over the prisoners and showered the pen with shrapnel and several shells fell onto the site without exploding, no serious injuries were inflicted. "[It] is trusting too much to the fuse to shoot two miles and expect the shell to burst 100 yards beyond the stockade," remarked prisoner Peter Akers. But the gunners were able to do just that. Most of the projectiles fell into Batteries Wagner and Gregg, killing Union troops and picking off guards outside the stockade and even on the parapet. But no Confederate POWs within the stockade were killed. Likewise, the Union POWs held throughout Charleston witnessed some close calls, but no serious injuries were suffered. After forty-four days the harrowing, nerve-racking experience for these POWs ended, but the Federal Government had already developed a new phase of retaliation, which none of them could escape.[64]

Chapter 9

"Sharply Hungry, Desperately Hungry—All the Time"

UNION RATIONS

With the latest string of executions and threats ending with the capture of Lee's son and the Morris Island POW group being returned to Fort Delaware, the Union began to fully implement a new stage of retaliation involving their entire POW population.

In the beginning the regulation ration decided upon by the authorities for prisoners of war was to be the same as that issued to the soldiers in the field. By that agreement, each prisoner was to receive three-fourths of a pound of bacon or one and one-fourth pounds of beef, one and one-third pounds of white bread or one and one-fourth pounds of corn bread, one-tenth pound of coffee, one and one-half ounces of rice or hominy, one-sixth pound of sugar, a gill of vinegar, a tablespoon of salt, an unspecified amount (depending upon what was available) of beans, potatoes, and molasses in small amounts, and one candle. The manner in which these rations was issued was left to the discretion of the commandant, so it varied from prison to prison. At some locations the daily specified amount of rations was divided up and issued three times a day while at other locations the specified amount was divided in half and issued twice a day—morning and evening. At still others, the rations were issued in bulk once every few days to be divided up and used at the discretion of each prisoner.[1]

The first prisoners, although uncomfortable in confinement, at least felt properly nourished. "I am as fat as I ever was," admitted prisoner John W.

Robison, after being confined at Camp Douglas Prison for several months after it was first established. "[T]he prisoners," added Thomas Head, 16th Tennessee Volunteer Regiment, also at Camp Douglas, "were supplied with more provisions than they were able to consume." Maj. Thomas Sparrow, a North Carolinian incarcerated at Fort Warren in late 1861 to early 1862, agreed. "[O]ur closet," he reported, "is never without crackers, cheese, bologna, sausages,—fruit cake, plain cake—coffee, [and] tea."[2]

Then, too, the prisoners were allowed to receive additional provisions sent to them from family and friends and to purchase additional items from local farmers and sutlers. "[W]e ordered daily supplies of meats, milk, and vegetables," reported one prisoner about his early confinement, "and with the addition of our rations, were enabled to live with reasonable comfort." And many other prisoners confined in Union military prisons early in the war agreed. "Our men having plenty of money live as well in the way of eating as we ever did," advised John Dooley, a Virginian confined at Johnson's Island.[3]

In fact, once a daily routine had been established at a number of prisons, several began to offer the captives special dining services, although at greatly inflated prices. At Fort Lafayette there was a special mess made available to the prisoners who could afford it by the Fort's ordnance sergeant, Anson Graves, 9th U.S. Infantry, and his family. For these meals prisoners were charged $1 per day credited against what the prisoners had turned over to prison authorities upon their initial arrival at the fort. "[He] supplies them with two meals a day for [$7] a week," one prisoner pointed out, "which is exorbitant for what they receive, ham and eggs for breakfast and eggs and ham for dinner." At Johnson's Island, Capt. Henry A. Gartrell of Georgia insists he spent, over a period of several weeks, $200 of his money for greasy soup made from old bones and other refuse, while prisoner Alonzo Cooper, confined at another Northern prison, said he had to pay $10 for nine sandwiches for himself and his messmates and later had to pay $5 for a small pie.[4]

But at some facilities, meals provided from the outside during this period were fairly priced and plentiful. "[A] sharp Yankee came down from Boston," reported a Fort Warren prisoner early in the war, "and proposed to draw our rations, and furnish us with two meals a day in good style, for one dollar per day." These meals often consisted of roast turkey, beef, ham, a variety of vegetables, "Yankee" pumpkin sauce, desserts, and even liquor. And, according to prisoner Lawrence Sangston, special feasts could be regularly purchased at a number of northern prisons during the winter of 1861. "[We] had a regular Yankee breakfast," he boasted in November 1861, "codfish and potatoes, baked beans and pumkin 'sass,'" and still later he noted in his journal: "Had an extra dinner at the mess today, being Sunday, roast turkies, roast and boiled mutton, roast beef and lobster salad, and dessert of nuts of several kinds, fresh peaches in cans, honey and coffee."[5]

But such elaborate meals were only available as long as the prisoners' money held out. By early to mid-1862 few could still afford such luxuries. Many, who had thought their imprisonment was only temporary and had lived lavishly for a time, now found themselves more dependent on the specified daily prison rations. "We are [now] here without clothing except that upon our backs and also without money to buy what we need," complained Lt. J. T. Menefee, 1st Alabama Infantry, in a letter from Camp Chase to his family on April 20, 1862. "I send you herewith authority to draw sufficient [funds] to buy, say, $50 in gold for me." Prisoner J. P. Jackson ran into the same problem by April 22. "When I was taken prisoner I had but little money; and now I have not [$1]," he wrote in a letter home, "and if you will send me some . . . you can hold my wages in the army, which is now $500. I am sure we could get the money that way." And yet another prison letter around that same period declared, "I hearby authorize and empower you to make out my pay account from the 31st of December, '61, to the 1st of May, '62. . . . This I hope you will do, as I need the money."[6]

But even faced with these hardships, many prisoners still considered their treatment fair during this period of their confinement and reflected as much in their letters, diaries, and journals.

"We draw ample rations and cook for ourselves," wrote prisoner J. B. Hall, "we are as well situated as prisoners could expect." Prisoner William O. Coleman agreed. "Rations are given to us just the same as to their own soldiers, perhaps a little better," he wrote in mid-1862. "With rations and what delicacies we buy, we live in fine style."[7]

"I am happy to say that we have nothing to complain of in regard to the treatment," Capt. J. L. Logan added in a letter he wrote to his wife from Camp Chase during this same period. "We are quartered in houses, with everything furnished us that we could ask for. . . . The greatest inconvenience I find is having no money that I can use."[8]

Col. William Hoffman, the Union commissary-general of prisoners, soon considered the specified amount of rations supplied to the prisoners excessive for men leading a sedentary life. After all, he reasoned—and his thinking was supported by Edwin Stanton of the War Department and Secretary William Seward of the State Department—these men were not marching or fighting as those in the field, so an equal amount of rations was unnecessary and costly. In addition, they figured, the prisoners could easily purchase their own food if they desired, saving the government even more. So, on July 7, 1862, barely one year after the Union took its first POWs, Hoffman ordered that rations be reduced at all Union military prisons and that the unissued portions be sold back to the commissary and the cash realized from these sales be placed in an established general prison fund. "The difference between the ration [provided the POWs] and the ration allowed by law to soldiers of the U.S. Army," instructed Hoffman, "constitutes the 'savings' from which is formed the 'prison fund.' . . . With this fund will be purchased all such articles as may be necessary for the health and comfort of the prisoners and which would otherwise have to be purchased by the Government."[9]

Authorities at the individual prisons generally made contracts with local dealers for their rations, which were then issued to the prisoners by a commissary at the camp. The ration expense at these facilities ranged from ten to fifteen cents per prisoner per day. Under this new plan the original specified amounts of meat, bread, rice, and beans was reduced while vegetables were regarded as "luxuries" to be purchased with money from the fund. The Union scheme was to pinch, scrimp, or hold back a portion of each individual ration issued to each prisoner at every issuance. Generally the ration savings were "mathematically" removed from the total to be distributed instead of actually physically removed and the withheld amounts were returned to the commissary for dollar credit and then added into future totals for redistribution later. There was no established set amount to be reduced from each ration. It was left to the discretion of the officials at each prison.[10]

"This is somewhat less than the allowance at present given under the recent commissary regulation," Capt. Henry M. Lazelle, assistant commissary general of prisoners, noted in a dispatch to Colonel Hoffman on July 28, 1862, after reviewing ration records and some of the reductions being made at one Union prison. "But I believe that it is more than enough for men taking little or no exercise."[11]

"A reasonable quantity of tobacco may be purchased, vegetables, etc., and any surplus after the purchase of necessaries will be used to purchase clothing, fuel, straw and in the payment of such incidental expenses consequent upon the care of prisoners which are now paid by the Government," added Colonel Hoffman. "It is not desirable to accumulate any large fund on hand," he cautioned, "nor is it intended to be wasted in the purchase of articles not necessary to the health and comfort of the prisoners or in the purchase of an undue quantity of luxuries."[12]

The Union plan also proposed to tax the prison sutler on the amount of business he did with the POWs and prohibited the prisoners from possessing money, urging that individual accounts or a system of vouchers be established so their purchases from the sutler could be deducted from the total amount of cash they had turned over to prison authorities upon entering the prison. At many prisons the sutlers issued token cards or scrip for the prisoners' use in making purchases. "All the money sent you by friends or relatives is deposited outside and you receive a receipt," complained prisoner R. F. Webb, 6th North Carolina Regiment, confined at Johnson's Island Military Prison when the new rule went into affect. "You are not allowed to use a cent of it. The sutler takes your name on his book with the amount due you from the outside and when you trade with him you sign a check or order for the amount. He will also give you fifty to seventy-five cents in checks or tickets with which to trade." This proposal then placed one additional limit on the captives. "We were prohibited from buying from any one except the sutler," complained prisoner J. H. George, confined at Johnson's Island.[13]

Throughout 1862 and on into 1863 the prisoners coped with their reduced rations the best they could and often supplemented their needs, out of necessity, with purchases from the high-priced sutler. Little notice was initially made of the Union's ration reduction in the many prisoner memoirs and letters of that period because within two weeks of implementing the controversial measure, both governments came to an agreement to exchange their POWs. Within the following months many of the facilities were nearly emptied out. With the collapse of the agreement several months later, however, the prison populations began to increase dramatically and the Union's "prison fund" reduction continued. "Our rations are not as good as they were a year ago, " complained one prisoner. "[I]t was difficult to make our scanty fare hold out," complained another, "and two thirds of the time I went to bed hungry."[14]

Many Southern men held in Northern prisons tended to agree. Although Union officials maintained that the portion of rations withheld from the prisoners for the prison fund was only "that [which] can be spared without inconvenience to them," the prisoners saw it quite differently. "For the first six months we had plenty to eat; coffee, beans, pork, and bread in sufficiency," reported a Rock Island prisoner. "[It] was about the middle of December [1863] when we started in to starve." Prisoner James F. Crocker, 9th Virginia Infantry, who became a POW in mid-September 1863, agreed. "When I first reached Johnson's Island," he recalled, "I found that the rations given to the prisoners, while plain, were good and abundant." By the end of the year he, too, found that conditions had worsened. In addition, because vegetables were seldom provided on a steady basis, scurvy began to appear in many of the Union prisons by November 1863. During these times, citizens living near the prisons often contributed fresh vegetables, but at times and at some prisons commandants saw no reason to allow prisoners to have them. Citizens in the vicinity of the Fort Delaware Prison were actually prevented from providing vegetables to the POWs held there and it was much the same at the facilities in New York. "[T]hey were not passed on to us," one Fort Lafayette prisoner bitterly complained upon learning civilians had brought vegetables to that prison. "We are denied every[thing] and are shut out from the world in this Bastille."[15]

No official percentage to reduce the rations was ever publicized by Union authorities, so the exact amount of food loss suffered by the prisoners during this period is unknown. Some contemporary Northern newspapers critical of the move estimated that prison officials had decreased the regular army ration by one-third. Secretary Stanton, himself, had originally proposed a reduction of 20 percent. Other sources have since estimated the figure to be more likely near 10 percent, but the exact amount varied from prison to prison. Then, too, as time went on, some facilities accumulated large amounts in the prison fund while others seemed to spend it as quickly as it collected.[16]

These prison funds, instead of being returned to Hoffman's Federal budget to be maintained and distributed, were established instead at each Union prison through the commissary so that each facility had its own account and merely reported the amount to the quartermaster general in Washington on a monthly basis. The original intent of this decision was to give the individual commandants control of the funds, believing they would know best how to benefit the POWs of their particular institution. In some cases the funds were properly managed and used to purchase vegetables and clothing or build hospitals and drainage systems, but in many prisons the fund eventually grew into staggering amounts that were never used and sometimes simply led to graft and corruption among the prison officials. At Camp Douglas, in Chicago, Illinois, for instance, over 4,400 POWs eventually died from the effects of the cold, a lack of clothing, and malnutrition, while Col. James A. Mulligan, one of the prison commandants, spent nothing on the prisoners but appropriated $1,500 from the fund for his own use and at this same prison, undercover detectives were paid $100 a month out of the fund to walk among the prisoners to spy on them. At Fort Delaware over $17,000 accumulated in the prison fund, yet prison officials refused to spend any of it on vegetables, while at least one of every eight Confederate prisoners suffered from scurvy. At Elmira Prison in New York officials falsified records to show portions of the fund were spent on the prisoners when the items listed were later determined to be nonexistent. And at the Union's Point Lookout Military Prison in Maryland, Federal agents eventually uncovered questionable spending practices of officials at that facility.[17]

During this period the prisoners' comfort was often sustained by the high-priced prison sutler or other outside sources. Eggs, milk, cheese, crackers, canned fruits, vegetables, boots, underclothing, and other items were available, but at exorbitant prices. Sutlers normally sold barrels of flour at twenty dollars a barrel, eight to ten dollars over market price, while bakers sold extra bread to the POWs for twenty-five to fifty cents a loaf, at nearly five times the market price, "[k]nowing that the famishing prisoners would be forced to buy at *any* price," as one prisoner explained. "And if occasionally the latter began to complain, the shop window was closed for a day or two [to both punish them and teach them a lesson]." With such price gouging after their reduction in rations, some prisoners became anxious while others became desperate. "I saw one poor fellow who had lost his mind for fear of starving to death," advised one prisoner. Another POW quickly summed up his situation in a letter home. "My Dear Dad," he wrote, "please send at once $100 or a coffin."[18]

Many prisoners who could not afford the sutler's high-priced provisions survived this period with the help of friends and relatives on the outside who provided boxes of food and clothing. By November 1863, however, Union authorities decided to place further restraints on their POWs. "I do not think it well to permit them to receive boxes of eatables from their friends," Hoffman advised his prison commandants in an official dispatch on November 9, "and I suggest you have them informed that such articles will not hereafter be delivered." To shut off all other possibility of the prisoners obtaining additional food beyond the rations issued by Union authorities, Hoffman then confided with his superiors and finally issued a follow-up order three weeks later. "By direction of the Secretary of War," he advised his prison commandants on December 1, "you will prohibit all trade with the sutler by prisoners of war."[19]

Informed of the order, the prisoners were furious but found there was little they could do. According to tabulations from the Official Records, however, there was a dramatic increase in escapes and attempts to escape at several Union prisons soon afterwards. At Alton Prison in Illinois twenty-three prisoners successfully fled during the month of November 1863 while sixty-five made it out of Camp Douglas. Another twelve successfully escaped from Point Lookout, Maryland, while twelve others eluded authorities and got away from Gratiot Street Prison in St. Louis the same month. In one apparent attempt to escape at Camp Douglas, a fire was started on November 11, soon after the package restriction was announced, that burned a barracks and a 400-foot section of the prison fence but the POWs were all forced back into other barracks at gunpoint. The following December six more escaped from Camp Douglas while twelve successfully fled Fort McHenry in Maryland and in the following month eighteen climbed over the wall at Camp Morton in Indiana.[20]

The following month, January 1864, Federal authorities, led by Secretary of War Edwin M. Stanton, hit the prisoners again with yet another daily ration reduction. "That order was approved by Abraham Lincoln," declared John A. Bateson, 8th Veteran Reserve, a Union guard at the Rock Island Military Prison at the time. "It was read at assembly for duty on the 2nd, in front of the prison [and] went into effect on the following day. . . . [I]t reduced the daily allowance of the captives to about ten ounces of bread and four ounces of meat per man."[21]

The situation deteriorated quickly in all the Northern prisons by the beginning of the new year. "Though our rations for the first two or three months were not to be complained of [and] the friends of the prisoners were allowed to furnish them with clothing and such things as they needed," revealed M. J. Bradley, Co. G, 10th Kentucky [Confederate] Infantry, held at Camp Douglas, "our rations were [soon] reduced to a small piece of tough beef or pickled pork and bread, with occasionally some beans and a little vinegar, and our condition was subsequently rendered intolerable." Horace Carpenter, 4th Louisiana Regiment, confined at Johnson's Island, agreed. "[The daily ration] was insufficient to satisfy the cravings of hunger and left us each day with a little less life and strength."[22]

With the elimination of vegetables, scurvy began to occur in epidemic proportions in many Union prisons by late 1863 and on into 1864. It was also during this period that the catching and eating of rats began in many of the facilities where they were abundant. It occured at Fort Delaware, Camp Chase, Johnson's Island, Camp Douglas, Point Lookout, Elmira, and a number of other locations.[23]

While such things were taking place in the North, the Confederate government was having its own problems feeding and maintaining the prisoners in their possession. The Confederate government had originally adopted the official U.S. Army ration upon the creation of its own army but, out of necessity, had to reduce it by the spring of 1862. In addition, on May 21, 1861, the Confederate Congress had passed an act declaring that their POWs would be fed exactly as their soldiers in the field but, again, began having problems living up to that intention almost immediately. "The question of food is daily becoming a more perplexing and dangerous one in the Confederate States," reported the *New York Times* as early as June 1861. "The lack of meat and bread may yet accomplish what reason and patriotism have failed to do."[24]

The report went on to compare the high prices of corn, flour, and pork, as just three examples, of the skyrocketing rates in the South in comparison with the North after just two months of war. Corn was selling for $.21 a bushel in Chicago to $.56 a bushel in New York while it was over $1.00 a bushel at Charleston and Montgomery. Pork was averaging $15.50 a barrel in Chicago to $16.50 a barrel in New York but was going for a whopping $26 in Montgomery and an unbelievable $27.50 a barrel at Charleston.

"In many of the Southern States," the *Times* continued, "the price of provisions is seen to be more than double what it is at the great depots of the North; so that in all such States where the Confederate Government have troops, they are costing as much to feed, as twice the number in arms are costing the North. . . . [I]f provisions are selling [in the South] at twice their usual price, [the Confederacy's] credit is exhausted with double the rapidity that might have been anticipated at the start."[25]

As time went on, conditions worsened across the South. Richmond authorities began moving large contingents of their prisoners to other locations where food seemed more abundant, but that too proved to be useless within a short time. In addition to an actual lack of supply caused by high prices, Confederate officials were increasingly confronted with immediate demands for the rations when they could be obtained. The Union army was moving through portions of the South, destroying everything in its path. This included confiscating or destroying livestock and crops, as well as the facilities for processing and transporting the livestock and crops. Many times after prison officials made the arrangements to provide enough rations for 1,500 captives at a given location, there were often over 2,000 or more incarcerated there by the time the supplies arrived, making it necessary to divide what arrived among more men. "If at any time there was privation among the prisoners at the South," insisted Confederate prisoner Harry Gilmore, held at Fort Warren in Boston Harbor later in the war, "it was caused by our poverty, not our will; the same scarcity frequently pinched our own soldiers." Rev. Thomas D. Witherspoon, chaplain, 42nd Mississippi Regiment tended to agree. "Whatever privations [the prisoners in the South] endured," he said, "were the privations of our own men, and were the result, not of willful neglect or bitter hatred, but of that dearth of the necessaries of life under which our whole people were suffering."[26]

It was true that shortly after the war's beginning the Confederate commissary department found itself impoverished and later, on several occasions, had to resort to forced confiscation just to provide the Confederate army. At the same time, authorities often impressed passing trains to provide for their POWs. It was done at Richmond and Salisbury, North Carolina, as well as at Andersonville, Georgia, as the war continued. By mid-1863 Confederate authorities were constantly arguing with Richmond's butchers and farmers over the availability of beef and pork while civilians were rioting in the city streets over the lack of food and the prices of what was available. "The 'Confeds' cannot feed their prisoners except just so far as to keep them alive," complained one Richmond prisoner on November 12, 1863. "The ration for officers is a piece of corn-cake six by four and one-half inches, and one inch thick, and one small sweet potato and water. This is everything for a day." Other Union soldiers imprisoned in the South agreed. "So long as they were able," said one, "they gave us good rations." He went on to point out that as the war continued he and other POWs often received "spoilt" bacon—cured with wood ashes because of the shortage of salt—or bad beef cured with saltpeter, or fresh horse meat when neither was available, because of the overall situation in the Confederacy. "The fare of our guards was not much better than our own," he admitted.[27]

But Union authorities disagreed. "[T]he treatment of our prisoners of war by the rebel authorities has been even more barbarous than that which Christian captives formerly suffered from the pirates of Tripoli, Tunis, and Algiers," argued General Henry W. Halleck. "[T]he horrors of 'Belle Isle' and 'Libby Prison' exceed even those of 'British Hulks' or the "Black Hole of Calcutta.' . . . It has been proposed to retaliate upon the enemy by treating his prisoners precisely as he treats ours. Such retaliation is fully justified by the laws and usages of war."[28]

Throughout November and December 1863, and on into early 1864, more and more reports continued to filter back to the north about Union troops suffering in the Southern prisons. The lack of enough food was the main complaint. As the reports continued, the press became involved, publishing numerous accounts, some true and some exaggerated, which aroused the public. Before long, the POWs' relatives and friends back home, as well as the politicians, began to cry out for retaliation. On April 20, 1864, Colonel Hoffman, at the encouragement of Secretary of War Stanton and Q.M. Gen. Montgomery C. Meigs, issued another order to further reduce rations in northern prisons in retaliation for the perceived neglect and wrongdoing of the Southern officials. After additional scrutiny, Colonel Hoffman contacted Secretary Stanton again on May 19. "[T]he ration as now issued to [our] prisoners of war," Hoffman suggested, "may be considerably reduced without depriving them of the food necessary to keep them in health." After conferring with others, Stanton endorsed the recommendation the following week. On the first day of June 1864, all Union prison commandants were advised to immediately put into effect the new retaliation reduction. Among other reductions and some complete eliminations, the original specified allowance of one and one-fourth pounds of beef was reduced to fourteen ounces while the original alternating issue of pork was reduced to ten ounces.[29]

"We are now beginning to feel to some extent the vengeance of the Government of the United States," complained one of the prisoners.

"They have stopped our rations of sugar, coffee and candles. We get nothing but bread and meat with a few beans."[30]

"[T]hey allowed us neither sugar, coffee, bacon, potatoes, or vegetables of any kind," added another prisoner, "and [we] were told by those in authority that this was in retaliation for what their prisoners were suffering in Southern prisons."[31]

"These orders put the prisoners on half rations," complained prisoner James F. Crocker. "The result of these orders was that the prisoners were kept in a state of hunger—I will say in a state of sharp hunger—all the time."[32]

Even with these reductions, however, complaints continued to generate throughout the North. "The maintenance of the mass of rebel prisoners we now have on our hands," complained the *New York Times,* "is costing the country something like $50,000 a day, or close to *twenty million dollars a year.*"[33]

Two months later the Union's June reduction was tightened up again, being superseded by yet another order which further reduced what could be obtained by Confederate POWs confined in Northern prisons. On August 10, Colonel Hoffman, by order of the secretary of war, eliminated any package deliveries to the prisoners, which had continued to be allowed to officers in some instances after the November 1863 order, and again restricted all trade with the prison sutlers, which had been relaxed somewhat for a short period of time after the original December closings. These actions completely cut off any possibility of obtaining food from other sources. The new regulations were more strictly adhered to and remained in effect throughout the remainder of the war. "It is not expected," Colonel Hoffman instructed his prison commandants, "that anything more will be done to provide for the welfare of rebel prisoners than is absolutely necessary, and in directing or recommending expenditures for their benefit you will have this constantly in mind." In effect, then, after late 1864 Confederate soldiers received nearly one-fourth the original established army ration—a mere handful of food—once a day. The biggest problem with these mandated reductions in the Union prisons was that the prisoners began to literally starve and were no longer able to properly manage the meager distributions. A vicious cycle of starving, eating, and starving again, quickly evolved. "The rations which were distributed at noon each day were expected to sustain life until the noon of the day following," complained Henry Shepherd, confined at Johnson's Island. "During this interval, many of us became so crazed by hunger that the prescribed allowance of pork and bread was devoured ravenously as soon as received. . . . For six or seven months I subsisted upon one meal [every] 24 hours."[34]

"Rations were issued to us every third day," advised George Moffett, held prisoner at Camp Chase during this period. "Once in a while, just to enjoy the novelty of a full stomach, we would eat up the three days' rations in one day, and then fast two. But experience taught us that that was an injudicious system, so the rule was [quickly learned] to spread out the short rations over the three days."[35]

"We [too] would at times become desperate for a full meal," agreed Crocker. "Then by common consent we would eat up our whole day's rations at one meal. And then, alas, we would get up with hunger—hungry still. My God, it was terrible!"[36]

"At Rock Island [after] the era of starvation was inaugurated," reported prisoner W. C. Dodson, 51st Alabama Cavalry, "for over twelve months my hunger was never appeased. . . . Rations for the day were issued each morning, and it was the custom to make but one meal and fast till the next morning. Saturday rations were issued for two days, and it was not uncommon for the men to eat all at once and do without until Monday."[37]

"I have seen men eat at one sitting all they drew for three days," insisted prisoner A. W. Sidebottom, "and take the chances of finding bones, catching rats, etc., to tide [them] over until rations were issued again."[38]

"I know from personal observation that many of my comrades died from starvation," insisted John A. Wyeth, Co. I, 4th Alabama Cavalry, held at Camp Morton, Indianapolis, Indiana, from late 1863 through 1864. "Day after day it was easy to observe the progress of emaciation until they became so weak that when attacked with an illness which a well-nourished man would easily have resisted and recovered from, they rapidly succumbed."[39]

The prisoners did begin to die at an alarming rate during this period. At Elmira Prison, 115 died in July 1864, its first month of operation, 385 in its second, and 276 in its third. Most of those POWs had been transferred in from Point Lookout Prison where another 432 died during the same period. At the same time, more than 250 succumbed at Rock Island Prison, 146 at Fort Delaware, 330 at Camp Douglas, and nearly 200 at

Camp Chase, as just a few other examples. The death totals remained high at many of the Union prisons in the later months of 1864 on into 1865.[40]

"Thousands of men were imprisoned and they were dying rapidly," recalled Rev. Malachi Bowden, Co. B, Georgia Infantry, imprisoned at Point Lookout in October 1864. "On my arrival, one of the first things I did was ascertain how many men were dying per day, and to calculate when my time would come, should I live to be the last survivor. The calculation showed that I would have but a short time to live."[41]

Bowden realized almost immediately that his survival in the prison would depend a lot on his diet. "Upon entering the prison," he continued, "I discovered several men of my company who had been captured before I was. They informed me that I could not live on the rations we drew there. I found our food to be a small cup of soup, with a stray Yankee bean in it here and there, and a piece of fat pickled pork. . . . This together with two or three cuts of loaf bread issued twice a day, completed our menu. They did allow us to draw a copious supply of vinegar. This I ate with my diet, and drank with water, hoping that it might help to keep down disease."[42]

Adding to the desperation, Union prisons, too, sometimes experienced problems with supply and demand. Similar to the situation experienced by officials of the Southern prisons, available rations in Union prisons had to be reduced to meet overall demand on several occasions at several facilities. When the allotted one-half to one-fourth rations had to be divided even more to stretch out among a greater number of prisoners who had arrived, prisoner complaints that their bean soup was nothing more than hot water "containing a bean or two" might not have been an exaggeration as many historians had once believed. Rations had to be reduced drastically at Fort Delaware on several occasions, issuing only hardtack three times a day during some periods, while a number of prisons issued no meat for several days in a row, and Camp Douglas ran out of food completely for six days during one period of 1864.[43]

Throughout 1864 and on into 1865 the Confederate prisoners in the Union prisons survived on the meager rations the best they could. "Often have I eaten my two day's rations at one meal," complained J. S. Kimbrough, Co. K, 14th Georgia, held at Hart's Island, New York, in late 1864, "and subsisted upon water and wind until the next drawing." Many prisoners sorely agreed. "There was just enough to keep the appetite whetted without satisfying it," said prisoner George Moffett. "It was just sufficient to maintain life yet leaving every one in a continual state of yearning hunger," offered another prisoner. Some of the prisoners caught and ate the dogs, cats, rats, and other animals that wandered into the facility. Others supplemented their diet the best they could. "I gave my pocket knife for a pie which had been seasoned with skimmings from the slop tubs at the cook house," admitted Point Lookout prisoner C. W. Jones, Co. H, 24th Virginia Cavalry, "for which I sorrowfully repented, for it gave me a spell of sickness which came very near sending me to the 'peach orchard' [cemetery], where many of the boys have gone." And still others sought help from the outside. "During this period of starvation," recalled Camp Douglas prisoner Thomas Head, "the prison was visited one day by some distinguished people from England. The prison officers were showing them around in great pomp. When they came to the barracks of [John Hunt] Morgan's men, the boys commenced crying out, 'Bread! bread! bread!' The British visitors looked confused and the prison officers were greatly exasperated. As a punishment, they ordered that no bread be issued to these men for the next twenty-four hours, and gave orders to all the men of the other barracks not to trade or traffic bread to those men under the severest penalties."[44]

Many of the POWs realized that they had become nothing more than pawns in this war and with the collapse of all exchange agreements between the two governments after mid-1863, there was nothing they could do but struggle to survive until the hostilities ended. For many, however, it became the cruelest struggle of the entire conflict.

"I said it then, and I have said it hundreds of times since," prisoner James F. Crocker later lamented, "that if I had an enemy whom I wished to punish exquisitely, I would give him just enough food to keep him in health with a sharp appetite, but not enough to satisfy his appetite. I would keep him hungry—sharply hungry, desperately hungry—all the time. It was cruel, bitter treatment."[45]

Chapter 10

"Crimes Which Disgrace the Age"

THE CRIMES OF WAR

When the American Civil War *did* finally come to an end, many prisoners of both sides were convinced they had been politically used throughout the conflict. Those who had been incarcerated in the South were angry, believing they had been deliberately starved by their captors and callously sacrificed by their own government, while those who had been confined in the North were just as angry, believing they had been held hostage and starved in retaliation. Friends and relatives of many deceased prisoners, and many newspaper editorials at the time, accused various government officials of conducting a campaign specifically calculated to reduce their enemy's ranks by limitless incarceration, starvation, and disease. More than 56,000 Union and Confederate POWs had died during confinement and untold thousands more were broken, sickly men when finally released.[1]

As the publicity, propaganda, and bitterness associated with the POWs reached new heights at war's end, the U.S. government moved quickly to bring charges against a number of Confederate government and prison officials. In addition to incarcerating Pres. Jefferson Davis, Vice Pres. Alexander Stephens, Secretary of War James Seddon, and even Howell Cobb, the Confederate major general commanding the District of Georgia, U.S. authorities rounded up and jailed Andersonville prison officials Capt. Henry Wirz, Capt. W. Sidney Winder, and Capt. Richard B. Winder; Maj. John H. Gee of Salisbury Prison; Lt. Col. John F. Iverson and Capt. Thomas G. Barrett

129

129

of the Florence facility; Maj. Thomas P. Turner and Richard Turner of
Libby Prison; George W. Alexander of Castle Thunder; and Capt. D. W.
Vowles of the Millen pen, among others. Full responsibility for conditions
at the most infamous Southern prison, Andersonville, fell on that prison's
commandant, Capt. Henry Wirz. He was brought to trial on war crimes before a special military commission in Washington, D.C., on August 23,
1865. Charged with conspiring with others to impair and injure the health
and destroy the lives of U.S. soldiers held under his authority—as well as
the deaths of thirteen specific prisoners of war—he was found guilty and
sentenced to death following a two-month trial. On November 10, 1865,
Henry Wirz was led to the gallows and, as Union soldiers and 250 ticket-
holding spectators chanted "Remember Andersonville!", he was hanged.
John Gee, the Salisbury, North Carolina, prison commandant was brought
to trial next. Arrested at his Quincy, Florida, home after the Confederate
surrender, Gee was incarcerated in Washington, D.C., until his trial began
in Raleigh, North Carolina. On February 21, 1866, Gee was brought before
a military commission and charged with "Violation of the laws and customs
of War" and "Murder in violation of the laws of War" regarding his man-
agement of the southern prison. After a four-month trial, Gee was finally
acquitted on all charges and released. Likewise, Iverson, Barrett, Vowles,
Sidney Winder, Richard Winder, and a number of others spent time in
prison but were never brought to trial. Most of these men were released by
mid-1866, after Gee's June acquittal and July release. Jefferson Davis, James
Seddon, and Howell Cobb had been originally named as coconspirators in
Wirz's original charge but were never brought to trial either. Seddon and
Cobb were released after five months imprisonment. Stephens was paroled
after six months and Jefferson Davis was not released until May 1867.[2]

For many of both sides who had survived the prisons, the experience
continued to be a devastating factor in their lives. Those who had endured
long periods of confinement often remained humiliated and bitter. They,
their families, and families who lost loved ones in the various facilities accused one or both governments of being deceitful or incompetent. The
blame, lies, accusations, vindictiveness, and propaganda as to who or what
was responsible for the starvation, cruelties, and prison deaths continued
for many years.

"It is admitted that the prisoners in our hands were not as well provided for as we would [have liked]," admitted Jefferson Davis, "but . . . we
did as well for them as we could. Can the other side say as much?"[3]

"Sufficient information has been officially published," insisted Robert E. Lee,

> to show that whatever sufferings the Federal prisoners at the South underwent were incident to their position as prisoners, and produced by the destitute condition of the country, arising from the operations of war. . . . It was the desire of the Confederate authorities to effect a continuous and speedy exchange of prisoners of war; for it was their true policy to do so, as their retention was not only a calamity to them but a heavy expenditure of their scanty means of subsistence, and a privation of the services of a veteran army.[4]

"[U]pon whom does this tremendous responsibility rest of all this sacrifice of human life, with all its indescribable miseries and sufferings?" asked former Confederate vice president Stephens.

> The facts . . . show that it rests entirely upon the authorities at Washington! It is now well understood to have been a part of their settled policy in conducting the war not to exchange prisoners. The grounds upon which this extraordinary course was adopted were that it was humanity to the men in the field, on their side, to let their captured comrades perish in prison rather than to let an equal number of Confederate soldiers be released on exchange to meet them in battle! . . . [Therefore] the false cry of cruelty towards prisoners was raised against the Confederates. This was but a pretext to cover their own violation of the usages of war in this respect among civilized nations.[5]

Stephens's reference was to the fact that the exchange of prisoners between the two sides had stopped simply because Federal authorities had recognized that the success or failure of the Union's war effort hinged on its supremacy in numbers. When exchanged earlier in the war, Confederate soldiers tended to rejoin their regiments more often than did the Federal soldiers. As a result, Federal authorities began to create excuses to stop further exchanges of prisoners in order to prevent Confederate soldiers from being released and rejoining the army.

"About the last of March, 1864, I had several conferences with General [Benjamin F.] Butler at Fortress Monroe in relation to the difficulties attending the exchange of prisoners and we reached what we both thought a tolerably satisfactory basis," declared Robert Ould, former Confederate commissioner of exchange in an article for the August 1868 *National Intelligencer.*

> The day that I left there, General Grant arrived. General Butler says he communicated to him the state of the negotiations and 'most emphatic verbal directions were received from the Lieutenant General not to take any step by which another abled bodied man should be exchanged until further orders from him'; . . . General Butler also, in an address to his constituents, substantially declared that he was directed . . . to put the matter offensively *for the purpose of preventing an exchange.*[6]

It was not learned until after the war that Butler, as soon as he was assigned as an exchange agent in late 1863, was *ordered* to use any excuse to avoid prisoner exchanges with the Confederacy. Confederate authorities became so desperate and willing to negotiate in order to rid themselves of the burden, responsibility, and concern for the health of the POWs in their possession that they even offered to resolve the controversy concerning black soldiers as POWs. "These questions were therein argued," admitted Butler, "not diplomatically, but obtrusively and demonstratively not for the purpose of furthering exchanges of prisoners, but for the purpose of preventing and stopping the exchanges and furnishing a ground on which we could fairly stand." In other words, no matter what the Confederate authorities offered or agreed to in proposing an exchange, Union authorities were determined to find some excuse to refuse. "I had determined," confessed Butler—who had become known throughout the Confederacy as both "Spoons," for his plundering of silverware and other valuables from Southern homes as his troops moved across the South, and "Beast Butler" for his repressive ironhanded rule during the Federal occupation of New Orleans and his involvement in a number of retaliation hangings in both

Louisiana and Virginia—"as a last resort, in order to prevent exchange, to demand that the outlawry against me should be formally reversed and apologized for before I would further negotiate the exchange of prisoners."[7]

In fact, it appears that Butler, so hated by the South and declared as an outlaw by President Davis, was actually appointed as the Union's special agent for exchange on December 17, 1863, by the Secretary of War *because* of the South's probable reluctance to deal with him. "You are doubtless aware that by proclamation of the President of the Confederate States Maj. Gen. B. F. Butler is under the ban of outlawry," Confederate agent Robert Ould advised Maj. Gen. Ethan A. Hitchcock, Union commissioner of exchange, several days after Butler was appointed.

> Although we do not pretend to prescribe what agents your Government shall employ in connection with the cartel, when one who has been proclaimed to be so obnoxious as General Butler is selected[,] self-respect requires that the Confederate authorities should refuse to . . . establish such relations with him as properly pertain to an agent of exchange. The proclamation of President Davis forbids that General Butler should be admitted to the protection of the Confederate Government, and he cannot therefore be received under a flag of truce. Accordingly, I am directed by the Confederate authorities to inform you that Maj. Gen. B. F. Butler will not be recognized by them as an agent of exchange.[8]

Confederate authorities continued to be reluctant to negotiate with Butler for several months, but eventually they became so desperate that negotiations began. "I reported the points of agreement between myself and the Rebel agent [Ould] to [Edwin Stanton] the Secretary of War," recalled Butler.

> The whole subject was referred by the Secretary of War to [U. S. Grant] the Lieutenant General Commanding, who telegraphed me on the 14th of April, 1864 . . . .: 'Break off all negotiations on the subject of exchange till further

orders.' . . . [T]herefore, all negotiations were broken off, save that [of] a special exchange of sick and wounded on either side. . . . On the 20th of April, I received another telegram of General Grant, ordering 'not another man to be given to the Rebels.'[9]

Butler's special exchange of the sick and wounded had been cleared through Stanton. Although the prisoners turned over to the Confederates were in comparably poor condition, Stanton quickly arranged for the worst cases received by U.S. authorities to be photographed and exhibited in front of a Congressional committee to aid the Lincoln administration's propaganda campaign. "There appears," said Stanton as he presented the prisoners to the committee, "to have been a deliberate system of savage and barbarous treatment and starvation." Stanton's innovative plan worked. First Congress, then the press, and then the public became outraged over the condition of the prisoners. Years later Butler would acknowledge he never believed the Federal prisoners were purposely ill-treated and admitted he and others were well aware at the time that the Confederate government couldn't supply their own soldiers with clothing, blankets, or anything more than corn bread, let alone adequately supply their prisoners. Still, Stanton insisted on retaliation and proposed the ration reduction for all the POWs in Union facilities. Commissioner Hitchcock objected to the proposal, saying it was inhumane. Others complained that such a plan was useless. "Apart from the objections which exist to the policy of retaliation," Union major general Daniel E. Sickles wrote President Lincoln, "it is at least doubtful whether it would inure to the benefit of our men, for the reason that the enemy are reported to be without the means to supply clothing, medicines, and other medical supplies even to their own troops." But Sickles was ignored while Hitchcock was overruled and the reductions were put into affect.[10]

Meanwhile, according to Butler, Grant remained convinced that any further exchanges of prisoners would only strengthen Lee's army and prolong the war. "[T]herefore," Butler wrote in his memoirs afterwards, "it was better that the prisoners then in confinement should remain so, no matter what sufferings would be entailed."[11]

"I did not deem it advisable or just to the men who had to fight our battles to reinforce the enemy with thirty or forty thousand disciplined troops at that time," insisted Grant. "An immediate resumption of exchanges would have had that effect without giving us corresponding benefits."[12]

"[T]his refusal to exchange was one of the most fatal blows dealt us during the war, and contributed to our overthrow more, perhaps, than any other single measure," admitted Judah P. Benjamin, former Confederate secretary of state. "I write not to make complaint of it, but simply to protest against the attempt of the Federals so to divide the consequences of their own conduct as to throw on us the odium attached to a cruelty plainly injurious to us, obviously beneficial to themselves."[13]

"From the very beginning the Confederate authorities were anxious to make arrangements for the exchange of prisoners," another southerner agreed. "I instructed General R. E. Lee to . . . seek an interview with General Grant to represent to him the suffering and death of Federal prisoners held by us," added Jefferson Davis, "and to urge in the name of humanity the observance of the cartel for the exchange of prisoners. To this, as to all previous appeals, a deaf ear was turned [and] the interview was not granted."[14]

"[With] the Federal Government remaining deaf to all appeals for exchange of prisoners," Confederate brigadier general John D. Imboden remarked,

> the incarceration of their captured soldiers could no longer be of any possible advantage to us . . . [indeed] they looked upon it as an advantage to them and an injury to us to have their prisoners in our hands to eat our little remaining substance. In view of all these facts . . . Generals [Howell] Cobb and [Gideon J.] Pillow and I were of one mind that the best thing that could be done was . . . to make arrangements to send off all the prisoners we had at Eufaula and Andersonville to the nearest accessible Federal post, and having paroled them not to bear arms until regularly exchanged, to deliver them unconditionally . . . [but] to my amazement the officer commanding the escort telegraphed back from Jacksonville that the Federal commandant at St. Augustine refused to receive . . . the prisoners.[15]

Once the war ended and many former POWs and their families learned these new details behind their imprisonment, it renewed the hatred and bitter feelings. Many Northern men who had been held in the South were angry that government officials had turned their backs on their plight and had abandoned them. Southern men who had been held in the North remained angry their captors had not only refused to exchange them but had sought to aggravate the situation by a vindictive retaliation upon them.

"I have received letters," admitted Butler, who was targeted with a lot of anger from both sides at the end of the war, "[saying I] 'left thousands of our brethren and sons to starve and rot in Southern prisons' [but] their blood does not stain my garments." A number of high-ranking southerners later agreed. "Without doubt Grant must be held responsible for the stoppage of the exchange of prisoners, which was the most cruel act of his plan of attrition," agreed former Confederate major general Dabney Herndon Maury. " No parallel can be found for this double crime against humanity. In order that two hundred thousand [sic] effectives should be kept from the ranks of the Confederate army, they were incarcerated and starved deliberately in Northern prisons while a greater number of his own men . . . were suffered to languish in Southern prisons."[16]

It would seem Grant was eventually left to take full responsibility for the controversial decision within just a few years of the war's end. Official records and crucial memoirs remain silent on the matter. Edwin Stanton fails to go into much detail, but he was quite active in the Union's war-policy decisions and favored harsh treatment of the South at war's end. Stanton, who became the target for much scorn and disdain immediately after the war for his support of ration reductions and the termination of exchanges, maintained that he and General Grant simply came to the realization that exchanges were potentially harmful to the Union at the same time and Stanton had merely supported Grant's policy. But if this was true, then why had Stanton personally suspended all exchanges by issuing General Orders No. 207 on July 3, 1863, revoking paroles and ordering all remaining unexchanged prisoners back into the field, while Major General Grant, unaware of the order, paroled his 30,000 POWs at Vicksburg on July 4 "for humanitarian reasons"? Indeed, the facts reveal that it was Stanton who had actually opposed the original exchange agreement between the two governments and then pointed out to the general, as soon as Grant received overall command, the benefits of stopping all prisoner exchanges with the South. At the same time, it was just as well-known that President Lincoln devoted much of his time and energy in the war effort, personally directing military movement and policy, and very early on made it clear that he, and he alone, would make the final decisions. Therefore, we must assume that the decision to do *anything* to prevent the exchange of prisoners was not one general's isolated decision but surely an agreed upon element of strategy within the administration to help bring the war to a close. Still, while many Northern officials remained mute on the subject to their deaths, there were others in the South who continued to argue over the issue of responsibility.

"It may be said that Grant's superiors adopted this cruel measure," insisted Maury, "[and] while I am ready to believe [it] was conformable with their war policy, I cannot resist the conviction that Grant could at any time have opened all those prisons, North and South, and have arrested the most cruel of all the horrors of this dreadful war."[17]

While Maury and many others remained convinced Grant could have easily ended the controversial policy, based on the few postwar memoirs that mention the matter, perhaps Grant couldn't. Considering the available evidence, it is quite possible General Grant simply fell on his sword for the Lincoln administration, and for Stanton in particular. "The suffering said to exist among our prisoners south was a powerful argument against the course [I] pursued," admitted Grant, still willing to take full responsibility for the decision years after the war, "and I so felt it."[18]

In addition to policies preventing prisoner exchanges and reducing prisoner rations, it is well to remember that the Lincoln Administration implemented another unprecedented measure earlier in the war by declaring certain medicines contraband when the president proclaimed the blockade of Southern ports in April 1861. Nearly all of the major pain relievers such as morphine and opium, and all the more commonly used treatment drugs such as calomel and quinine, came from overseas at the time. Once declared contraband these badly needed medical items became increasingly scarce in the South. As a result, the Federal blockade caused suffering among Union prisoners as well as Southern soldiers. "[W]henever they found medicine on a blockade runner it was confiscated," reported Edward W. Boate, Co. K, 42nd New York. "[It was] a policy which indicated, on the part of our rulers, both ignorance and barbaric cruelty." L. H. Crawford, Co. A, Gray's South Carolina Cavalry Brigade, bitterly agreed.

"The Federal Government," he said, "is the only government ever known to have resorted to such harsh means."[19]

A number of European nations and even many Northerners considered this policy just as inhumane and callous as the administration's other two policies. Dr. W. H. Gardner, U.S. Army, assistant surgeon, of New York, pleaded at the 1863 Chicago convention of the American Medical Association for the Federal government to at least remove medicinal plant agents from the contraband list but he was booed and hissed by a majority of those present. "He [also] introduced a preamble and resolutions to petition the Northern government to repeal the orders declaring medical and surgical appliances contraband of war," recalled Dr. Samuel E. Lewis of Washington, D.C., who was present, "arguing that such cruelty rebounded on their own soldiers, many of whom as prisoners in the hands of the Confederates shared the suffering from such a policy, while the act itself was worthy of the dark ages of the world's history." Consequently, Gardner was hissed and continually interrupted until he left the hall. "[A]s these same drugs and medicines would also be applied to the relief of our own sick soldiers," complained L. M. Park of LaGrange, Georgia, "[the U.S. government and others] determined it would be to their advantage to let all die alike."[20]

The blockade is said to have been suggested by William H. Seward, Lincoln's secretary of state. The U.S. secretary of the navy, Gideon Welles, was against the measure and urged the president to simply close the Southern ports by executive order, instead. But Lincoln and Seward knew that by declaring a formal blockade, the U.S. government would then have the right, under international law, to stop and search neutral merchant ships on the high seas and to confiscate any declared contraband of war bound for Confederate ports.[21]

Although there was always some dissension among cabinet members and other Union government authorities each time one of these measures was proposed, Lincoln ultimately put the policy into effect over their objections. Adverse public opinion, too, was similarly ignored. "[T]he Secretary has taken and obstinately held a position of cold-blooded policy, (that is, he thinks it policy) in this matter, more cruel than anything done by the secessionists," complained renowned poet Walt Whitman, in an angry letter to the *New York Times*.

The Secretary has also said (and this is the basis of his course and policy) that it is not for the benefit of the Government of the United States that the power of the secessionists should be repleted by some 50,000 men in good condition now in our hands . . . [and] Major General Butler, in my opinion, has also incorporated in the question of exchange a needless amount of personal pique and an unbecoming obstinacy. . . . In my opinion, the anguish and death of these ten to fifteen thousand American young men, with all the added and incalculable sorrow, long drawn out, amid families at home, rests mainly upon the heads of members of our own Government.[22]

Granted, they sometimes allowed other officials to take the full brunt of the blame and criticism; however, it is apparent Lincoln and Stanton both realized that winning a modern war required not just defeating the enemy in various battlefield engagements, but it also involved the total destruction of its resources. This would include its railroad lines, its crops, cattle, pigs, and other food sources, its mills, granaries, and other food production and transportation facilities, and no matter how, one way or another, even its manpower. "In using the strong hand, as [we are] now compelled to do," Lincoln once contemplated, knowing full-well what would be required of his cabinet, "the government has a difficult duty to perform."[23]

Throughout the war Stanton was perceived as highly vindictive and afterwards paid the price in public opinion. Lincoln's demeanor, on the other hand, remained more aloof, through privately he was just as vehement. Since then, it has been asserted that the Union president was merely playing up to the overwhelming public opinion at the time but that he was just as much against the original prisoner exchange cartel of July 22, 1862, as Stanton and afterwards encouraged him to find reasons not to honor the agreement. Whoever was actually responsible, the reasons were quickly found, and Lincoln, who always said he, and he alone, would make the final decision, was able to remain above the controversy.[24]

In fact, the Northern president remained above the fray as each controversial decision was made. In March 1863, Stanton and Edward Bates, Lincoln's attorney general, consulted with Francis Lieber, a law professor at

Columbia University who was an expert on the U.S. Constitution and highly knowledgeable in international law, to help codify the rules of war. In truth, the so-called rules of war had been established long before the American Revolution, but the Lincoln administration needed an official interpretation slanted more toward their needs: a policy, they said, for co-ordinating ground warfare as well as to cover the military occupation and restoration of national authority in certain areas. This eventually led to the creation of the Union's General Orders No. 100, which became known as the Lieber Code.[25]

Francis Lieber had immigrated to America from Prussia in the 1840s. He first settled in Charleston and taught at South Carolina College before moving to New York in 1856 and teaching at Columbia. He became widely known for his expertise on the U.S. Constitution and for his lectures on the principles of individual rights. In 1861 he was chosen to confer an honorary Doctor of Letters on Lincoln. As a result of that meeting, early in the war Bates had approached him on the administration's behalf to help find precedents to justify the president's actions regarding political arrests and the suspension of the writ of habeas corpus. Although Lieber doubted the legality of Lincoln's actions at the time, he was able to find and develop a logical defense. In August of 1862, after the U.S. Congress passed the Confiscation Acts, Stanton asked Lieber to prepare a treatise on the needs and legality of fugitives coming to the armies for support and protection and employment of blacks in the Union army. Again, he came through for the Lincoln officials. So, by 1863, Lieber had become an unofficial adviser to the Lincoln administration and a devoted member to the Union cause—even though he had sons in both armies.[26]

The Lieber Code, promulgated as General Orders No. 100 by President Lincoln on April 24, 1863, contained 157 articles addressing everything from martial law and military jurisdiction, to prisoners of war and hostages, partisans, spies, captured messengers, and traitors, up to and including the exchange of prisoners and the armistice. The code was purposely written in sometimes vague or confusing language, which contained some contradictions. In this way it accomplished the administration's goals yet presented a humane atmosphere to satisfy the general public. "To save the country is paramount to all other considerations," declared the code in plain unequivocal language. "War is not carried on by arms alone," it noted. "It is lawful to starve the hostile belligerent, armed or unarmed, so that it leads to the speedier subjection of the enemy." But when the code began to address the issue of retaliation, it became conveniently vague and contradictory. "A reckless enemy often leaves to his opponent no other means of securing himself against the repetition of barbarous outrage," it declared. "Retaliation will, therefore, never be resorted to as a measure of mere revenge, but only as a means of protective retribution, and moreover, cautiously and unavoidably; that is to say, retaliation shall only be resorted to after careful inquiry into the real occurrence, and the character of the misdeeds that may demand retribution." As if that wasn't confusing enough, it then addressed retaliation on POWs. "A prisoner of war is subject to no punishment for being a public enemy," declared Article 56, "nor is any revenge wreaked upon him by the intentional infliction of any suffering, or disgrace, by cruel imprisonment, want of food, by mutilation, death, or any other barbarity." But three articles later the Lieber Code seemed to cover all aspects by declaring, "All prisoners of war are liable to the infliction of retaliatory measures." Then Article 109 of the order continued to further aid the Union cause by declaring, "A cartel is voidable as soon as either party has violated it."[27]

It was also the Lieber Code that led to the arrests of numerous Confederates who attempted to recruit behind Union lines. "Scouts, or single soldiers," declared the code, "if found within or lurking about the lines of the captor, are treated as spies, and suffer death." And it was under this code that Union authorities proceeded to clear the country-side of guerrilla fighters. "Partisans are soldiers armed and wearing the uniform of their army," declared Article 81, "but belonging to a corps which acts detached from the main body for the purpose of making inroads into the territory occupied by the enemy. If captured, they are entitled to all the privileges of the prisoner of war." The Code, however, then went on to say, "Men, or squads of men, who commit hostilities . . . without being part and portion of the organized hostile army . . . if captured, are not entitled to the privileges of prisoners of war, but shall be treated summarily as highway robbers or pirates." These "armed enemies not belonging to the hostile army" were more often referred to as irregulars. The term "bushwhackers" was applied to Confederate irregulars who committed raids into Union-held territory to kill and loot. Union irregulars who did the same in Southern territory were referred to as "jayhawkers." Occasionally such guerrilla warfare did operate indifferently to political sympathies and conducted raids no different than bandits in those areas, but military authorities of both sides often publicly deplored the existence of these "outlaws," while making use of them whenever possible—even rewarding them with military commissions. The problem was those who were regarded as guerrillas or irregulars by one side were often regarded as an integral part of operations by the other side. Good examples would be the Kirk brothers of Tennessee. Although the Confederacy regarded them as insurrectors and nothing but a protagonistic band of guerrillas, the Federal government regarded them as part of their mountain operations whose style of raiding and fighting was necessary in the region in which they had to operate. The same was true with Confederates John Hunt Morgan operating in the Ohio Valley, M. Jeff. Thompson in the Missouri Valley, and William Quantrill in the Trans-Mississippi region. These men were all considered nothing more than raiders and outlaws by Federal authorities, but they all eventually received official commissions in the Confederate army while they conducted the effective form of warfare necessary in the regions they operated. "[O]ur guerrilla fighting in Missouri must now give place to a different mode, that of regular, systematized warfare," Confederate general Sterling Price was advised in December 1861, in a clear indication that such operations had become a necessary stage of Confederate warfare. What is interesting, with all the disdain and scorn later displayed by Union officials over the Confederate use of irregulars in the war it was actually the Union who first sanctioned their use when the Unionist jayhawkers out of Kansas invaded Missouri.[28]

It seems by late 1863 or early 1864 the Union government had succeeded in their efforts to convince a majority of Northerners that the Confederacy and the Southern people required not only complete destruction to be defeated, but in fact deserved it. "In pushing up the Shenandoah Valley," Lt. Gen. Ulysses S. Grant advised Maj. Gen. David Hunter, "it is desirable that nothing should be left to invite the enemy to return. Take all provisions, forage, and stock wanted for the use of your command [and] such as cannot be consumed destroy." Such orders were continually passed down the line in the ensuing months. "Destroy all mills, all grain and forage," General Sheridan ordered Brig. Gen. Wesley Merritt, "drive off or kill all stock, and otherwise carry out the instructions of Lieutenant-General Grant, an extract of which is sent you, and which means, 'leave the Valley a barren waste.'" The devastation and destruction became increasingly systematic among the Union troops throughout the South. "We have . . . consumed the corn and fodder in the region of country thirty miles on either side of a line from Atlanta to Savannah, as also the sweet potatoes, cattle, hogs, sheep and poultry, and have carried away more than 10,000 horses and mules, as well as a countless number of their slaves," Sherman boasted in December 1864, as he summarized his Savannah campaign and March to the Sea for his Chief of Staff, Gen. Henry Halleck. "I estimate the damage done . . . at $100,000,000; at least $20,000,000 of which has inured to our advantage, and the remainder is simple waste and destruction. This many seem a hard species of warfare, but it brings the sad realities of war home. . . . As to the rank and file . . . they 'did some things they ought not to have done.'"[29]

Throughout the war the Union government maintained that since it was the Confederate forces who committed the first unlawful killing of prisoners, the North only acted in retaliation. At the same time, the Confederacy blamed Federal troops for beginning "the awful vortex into which things [were] plunging." Ironically, both sides could point out evidence to back their claims. Although the execution of Confederate soldiers at St. Louis's Gratiot Street Prison was in retaliation for the murder of Union major James Wilson and six of his command, their initial killing was possibly in retaliation for six men and an officer of Reves's command who were not given quarter by Wilson's troops when captured near Doniphan, Missouri, several miles south of Pilot Knob several days before. In addition, although the general public remained completely unaware of it until well after the war, Major Wilson and his troops had rode down upon a group of soldiers from the 15th Missouri (Confederate) Cavalry Regiment who were holding Christmas services with their families at a farm in southwest Ripley County, Missouri, on the morning of December 25, 1863. Surrounding the group, Wilson's command killed a number of the soldiers, captured others wounded too badly to escape, and killed many civilian men, women, and children in what became known locally as the Wilson Massacre. Although, officially, the Union army regarded Reves and his men guerrillas, who under the Lieber Code, were not entitled to the privileges of a prisoner of war if apprehended, according to Confederate authorities Reves officially commanded the 15th Missouri Cavalry Regiment, C.S.A., with the rank of captain, making his men entitled to such treatment. It was no wonder, then, that Reves regarded Wilson and the 3rd Missouri State Militia with such hatred. Similar incidents were responsible for a number of retaliations back and forth all across the warring nation. One of the more infamous occurred at Front Royal, Virginia, when six of Lt. Col. John Singleton Mosby's men, members of what the Confederacy officially recognized as the 43rd Virginia Cavalry Battalion, were coldly executed in the center of town by Federal troops after they surrendered. Four of the men were shot and two were hanged, and afterwards labels were pinned to their bodies which read, "Such is the fate of all of Mosby's men."[30]

"Why should the members of the 43rd Virginia Battalion have been singled out?" demanded Confederate major A. E. Richards. "Their mode of warfare did not depart from that of a civilized nation, the prisoners captured by them had always been humanely treated . . . they were executed solely because they were members of Mosby's command."[31]

Union troops regarded Mosby and his men as guerrillas or partisan rangers and irregulars, undeserving of POW status. Because of Mosby's success and domination over the Piedmont region of Virginia, Lieutenant General Grant had instructed Major General Sheridan to execute "without trial" all of Mosby's men whenever they were apprehended. Sheridan, in turn, passed the order down the line through Bvt. Maj. Gen. Wesley Merritt's divisions, commanded by Brig. Gen. Thomas C. Devin, Bvt. Maj. Gen. George A. Custer, and Maj. Gen. George Crook. Although others had been captured and killed the previous month by other divisions, those at Front Royal were captured by members of Col. Charles Russell Lowell's brigade under Custer. It was George Custer who ordered their execution and Lowell's command, composed of the 2nd Massachusetts, who carried it out. The following month, after obtaining the approval of Gen. Robert E. Lee and James Seddon, the Confederate secretary of war, Mosby retaliated by shooting and hanging a similar number of Federal prisoners, members of Companies G and L of the 5th Michigan Cavalry. Mosby left the bodies along the Valley Turnpike, Sheridan's main highway of travel through the region, with notes pinned on them declaring it was in retaliation for those at Front Royal, and further adding that retaliation would continue "measure for measure."[32]

The same can be said of the "Palmyra Massacre," as it came to be known. Although contemporary and postwar accounts of the Palmyra incident fail to associate the killing of Allsman—which led to the Palmyra execution—to any prior incident in the area, there is ample evidence to suggest Allsman, a Union man, might have been killed in retaliation for the execution of John L. Owen, a Confederate, the previous June.

"Colonel Owen, it appears from the account given in the Missouri papers . . . was shot without trial," Gen. Robert E. Lee complained in a dispatch to Union major general George B. McClellan. "He was a commissioned officer of the [2nd] Division of the Missouri State Guard [CSA]. . . . If Colonel Owen entered your lines in disguise we cannot deny your right to try and punish him. But his execution without trial is not considered justifiable."[33]

According to the Hannibal [Mo.] *Herald,* Owen was a "notorious rebel outlaw" who had made himself "conspicuous" by burning bridges, railroad cars, depots, and firing into passenger troop trains in the region. He had been hunted by Union troops for the past year and was finally captured by Company A, 11th Missouri State Militia, under the command of Lt. John Donahoo, near the farmhouse of his mother, Nancy Owen, outside Monroe, Missouri, about twelve miles southwest of Palmyra, on Saturday morning, June 7. "He begged the soldiers to take him prisoner," the *Herald* blatantly reported. "They informed him that 'taking prisoners' was played out. They then placed him upon a stump in front of a file of soldiers and at the word of command eight bullets pierced the body of the rebel, killing him instantly. Thus has ended the career of a notorious bushwhacker and outlaw. He has met the just retribution of his damning crimes."[34]

Owen had been killed as his mother, two brothers, his wife, Mary, and their child had watched in horror from the house. Afterwards the soldiers forced their way into the home, ransacked it, arrested John's brothers, Amsley and William, and shoved the other family members around before leaving. On July 3, Mary Owen wrote a letter to the Quincy [Ill.] *Herald* denying the accusations against her husband, complaining of his murder and the treatment the family received. Her letter was printed along with a strong editorial condemning the Union soldiers for "cold-blooded murder." "If he had been shot in the actual perpetration of any of the crimes alleged," declared the *Herald,* "he would have received but his just desert."[35]

"This letter has caused the murder of at least one Union man, a very estimable citizen named Pratt, of Lewis County," Palmyra's provost marshal, William R. Strachan, bitterly complained in a dispatch to Gen. John M. Schofield, commanding the District of Missouri, and further referring the matter to Col. John McNeil, "and the letter has been seized as a holy thing by all the traitors in our section. Its appeal for assassinations has done irreparable mischief already—it has continually aided and comforted the opponents of the Government." Strachan went on to write letters to the Quincy *Whig*, a pro-Union newspaper in the region, defending the actions of the troops stating the general order, signed by Maj. Gen. John Pope, which commanded Owen to be shot when apprehended, was properly read to him "and he was regularly executed in accordance with military usage."[36]

Before long, the Union general-in-chief Henry Halleck and George W. Randolph, the Confederate secretary of war at the time, also became embroiled in the controversy as additional "assassinations" and executions sporadically occurred throughout the region. "[Y]ou were instructed by the Secretary of War to make inquiries of the general commanding the U.S. forces relative to alleged murders committed on our citizens by officers of the U.S. Army," Pres. Jefferson Davis reminded General Lee. "We have since been credibly informed that numerous other officers of the armies of the United States have within the Confederacy been guilty of felonies and capital offenses which are punishable by all law human and divine. A few of those best authenticated are brought to your notice. . . . [Since no answer has been received,] you will further give notice that in the event of our failure to receive a reply to these inquiries within fifteen days from the delivery of your letter we shall assume that the alleged facts are true and are sanctioned by the Government of the United States. In such event, on that Government will rest the responsibility of the retributive or retaliatory measures which we shall adopt to put an end to the merciless atrocities which now characterize the war waged against us." Completely ignoring the inquiries, Union officials continued to conduct their regular operations in the region. Within two weeks, the Union colonel John McNeil authorized the execution of sixteen privates and one Confederate colonel in Kirksville, Missouri, and several more in Macon City, Missouri, shortly thereafter, all of which would eventually build toward a climax the following month with the disappearance of Allsman and the Palmyra execution.[37]

Of course, Confederate officials and Southern soldiers weren't entirely innocent of similer occurrences. Their deeds were simply overshadowed by a much larger, more powerful foe. Such events of *lex talionis* developed almost immediately at the very beginning of the conflict. Confederate officials in Texas retaliated against Federal soldiers in the very beginning months of the conflict in 1861 when Union troops were preparing to evacuate under an agreement of free passage out of the state. Concentrating their forces at Green Lake—the largest body of fresh water near the coast that could support a large encampment until ships arrived to transport the Union troops out of Texas—Confederate authorities worried the site had become too well-fortified and prevented their recruiting of its experienced soldiers. With the firing on Fort Sumter in South Carolina in April, Confederate authorities revoked their original agreement to allow an undisturbed exodus and moved quickly to recruit those remaining at Green Lake. All the Union soldiers who refused to enlist in the Confederate army were retaliated against by being seized and incarcerated as prisoners of war. But many examples of violent retaliations sprang up just as quickly. "[T]he rebels took three Indiana boys prisoners and turned around and ran the bayonet through their heads," declared David Hall, Co. E, 3rd Ohio Regiment, conducting operations in West Virginia in September 1861. "The Indiana boys swore that they will never take another prisoner: that they would serve them [the Confederates] like they did them."[38]

Although most of the retaliatory measures during the war were possibly initiated by individual commanders in the field, only to be reluctantly sanctioned by their respective governments afterward, official records and other sources do show that an overwhelming number of major retaliation incidents, such as prison executions, placing POWs under fire, and reducing their rations, were actually promoted, if not encouraged, by higher government authorities. At the same time, the trail of paperwork for retaliatory executions in the field quite often directly implicated official involvement of the two governments as well. "[This war] has transformed the very natures of the men engaged in it," chastised the *New York Times* in agreement. "From its very incipient stage it has been a master passion, which has fired every soul, high and low, with a wickedness almost infernal."[39]

Similar to the heated passions found in Missouri, Kentucky, Tennessee, and Virginia, the situation in the Gainesville area of Texas or the Shelton Laurel area of North Carolina was no different. McNeil, Burnside, Sherman, Custer, Keith and Bourland, and many others, never denied their roll in the executions and killings. They just denied that the murders were war crimes. Instead of today's ethnic cleansings, these might be called "political cleansings," for they definitely eradicated or at least silenced opposition in the areas where they were committed. The same was true in holding Michael Corcoran and the others, including Sawyer, Flinn, Rooney Lee, and Brig. Gen. Neal Dow as hostages in chains while threatening their lives. Desperate authorities justified such action if it prevented the executions of others—believing they were doing what was right and necessary in their circumstances. And, after all, even Lincoln, Stanton, Meigs, Halleck, and Hoffman all believed or at least authorized and signed off on the order to reduce prison rations, apparently believing it necessary and justified. "We of the North are, beyond all question, right in our lawful cause," insisted Gen. William T. Sherman. "We must make the people feel that this species of warfare can have but one result—utter ruin to their country." Through a continuation of bitter lies, cover-ups, and propaganda, Union officials successfully continued to wage war against the South years after its surrender, shifting all the blame for the war's cruelty, vengeful policies, and loss of life on the Confederate government authorities and its prison officials. "The pulpits, the press and the Government reports were so busy denouncing 'Rebel Barbarities,'" complained one Southerner, "that they had no censure for the McNeils, the Turchins, the Butlers, the Milroys, the Hunters, the Shermans, and the Sheridans, who, under the flag of 'Liberty,' perpetrated crimes which disgrace the age."[40]

"[L]ike all feuds," one veteran later observed, "it brought about an excitement well calculated to impair the mind, dethrone reason, and cause men to do things that [afterward], when the excitement had passed away, they greatly regretted. . . . I have heard men say when the war between the states came up, and they went into it, and got the war excitement up, they did things they could not have believed that they ever would have done."[41]

Notes

INTRODUCTION

1. See U.S. War Department, *War of the Rebellion: A Compilation of the Official Records of the Union and Confederate Armies* (Washington, D.C.: Government Printing Office, 1894–1899), series II, vol. 1, 92–93 and 104, hereafter referred to as *O.R.*; D. U. Barziza, *Decimus et Ultimus Barziza: The Adventures of a Prisoner of War, 1863–1864,* ed. R. Henderson Shuffler (Austin: University of Texas Press, 1964), 91.

2. Lonnie R. Speer, *Portals to Hell: Military Prisons of the Civil War* (Mechanicsburg, Pa.: Stackpole Books, 1997), xviii, hereafter referred to as Speer, *Portals to Hell.*

3. *O.R.,* series 2, vol. 3, 6.

4. Ibid., vol. 6, 649.

5. Ibid., ser. 1, vol. 33, 867.

6. Ibid., ser. 2, vol. 3, 885.

7. *New York Times,* Nov. 19, 1861.

8. James Kent, *Commentaries on American Law,* vol. 1 (New York: W. Osborn, 1844), 125.

9. William Edward Hall, *Treatise on International Law* (Oxford, England: Clarendon, 1884), 304.

10. *New York Times,* Dec. 1, 1862.

11. *O.R.,* ser. 2, vol. 4, 350.

12. Ibid., 552.

13. Ibid., vol. 1, 231.

14. Ibid., vol. 8, 387–88.

15. Ibid., vol. 4, 473.

16. Ibid., ser. 1, vol. 43, 811.

17. Ibid., 822.

18. Ibid., vol. 27, 930.

19. Ibid., vol. 32, 280–81.

20. Ibid., vol. 43, 910.

CHAPTER 1

1. St. Louis *Daily Democrat,* October 20, 1864; O.R. ser. 1, vol. 41/4, 657; Cyrus A. Peterson, *Narrative of the Capture and Murder of Major James Wilson* (St. Louis: A. R. Fleming, 1906), 10–12.

2. Ibid.

3. St. Louis *Daily Democrat,* Oct. 29, 1864.

4. Speer, *Portals to Hell,* 14.

5. The following account of the fate of Wilson and his men at the hands of Crisp and Reves comes from the St. Louis *Daily Democrat* for Oct. 29, 1864.

6. *New York Times,* Oct. 28, 1864.

7. *St. Louis Daily Democrat,* Oct. 31, 1864.

8. Ibid.

9. Ibid.; *St. Louis Daily Democrat,* Oct. 30, 1864.

10. Ibid.

12. *St. Louis Daily Democrat,* Oct. 29, 1864.

13. Ibid.

14. The details of the inquiry and the following quotes of testimony are taken from the issues of the *St. Louis Daily Democrat,* Oct. 30 and 31, 1864.

15. *O.R.,* ser. 2, vol. 7, 1111, 1115, 1118–19.

CHAPTER 2

1. *New York Times,* Aug. 11, 1861.

2. *Confederate Veteran,* 17 (1909): 333.

3. William H. Jeffrey, *Richmond Prisons, 1861–62* (St. Johnsbury, Vt.: Republican, 1893), 7, hereafter referred to as Jeffrey, *Richmond Prisons.*

4. Ibid., 8.

5. Ibid.

6. Ibid., 9.

7. J. Lane Fitts, "Ten Months in Confederate Prisons," in Jeffrey, *Richmond Prisons,* 129, hereafter referred to as Fitts, "Ten Months."

8. *Washington, (D.C.) Daily National Intelligencer,* Oct. 17, 1861; *O.R.,* ser. 2, vol. 4, 394; Michael Corcoran, *The Captivity of General Corcoran: The Only Authentic and Reliable Narrative of the Trials and Suffering Endured during his Twelve Months Imprisonment in Richmond and Other Southern Citiex* (Philadelphia: Barclay, 1865), 62, 64, hereafter referred to as Corcoran, *Captivity.* His attendant's name was John Owens.

9. *Washington (D.C.) Daily National Intelligencer,* Oct. 17, 1861.

10. Fitts, "Ten Months," 112.

11. Corcoran, *Captivity,* 27, 30.

12. Ibid., 29.

13. Ibid., 27.

14. Ibid., 39, 40.

15. Ibid., 39–40; Alfred Ely, *Journal of Alfred Ely: A Prisoner of War in Richmond,* ed. Charles Lanman (New York: D. Appleton, 1862), 109, hereafter referred to as Ely, *Journal.*

16. Corcoran, *Captivity,* 46.

17. Ibid., 40.

18. *O.R.,* ser. 2, vol. 3, 6, 692; William B. Hesseltine, *Civil War Prisons: A Study in War Psychology* (Columbus: Ohio State University Press, 1930), 13.

19. *O.R.,* ser 2, vol. 3, 738–39. The trials of the *Savannah* crewmen had been delayed for four months as legal manuvering took place. In fact, during this time their attorney, Algernon Sydney Sullivan, was ordered arrested by Secretary of State Seward, causing Sullivan to be incarcerated in Fort Lafayette as a political prisoner charged with "aiding, abetting, and communicating with the enemy"—a result of him talking with his clients! Ann Middleton Holmes, *Algernon Sydney Sullivan* (New York: New York Southern Society, 1929), 43–44.

20. *O.R.,* ser. 2, vol. 3, 131–32.

21. Ely, *Journal,* 212.

22. Ibid.

23. Corcoran, *Captivity,* 50, 52.

24. *O.R.,* ser. 2, vol. 3, 738.

25. William C. Harris, *Prison-Life in the Tobacco Warehouse at Richmond*

by a Ball's Bluff Prisoner (Philadelphia: George W. Childs, 1862), 103, hereafter referred to as Harris, *Prison-Life*.

26. *O.R.,* ser. 2, vol. 3, 739.

27. Harris, *Prison-Life*, 104.

28. Corcoran, *Captivity,* 50.

29. *New York Times,* Dec. 31, 1861; *O.R.,* ser. 2, vol. 3, 242.

30. *Charleston Mercury,* Nov. 12, 1861.

31. *New York Times,* Aug. 21, 1861.

32. *Charleston Mercury,* Nov. 12, 1861.

33. *New York Times,* Dec. 31, 1861.

34. *O.R.,* ser. 2, vol. 3, 127.

35. Ibid., 776.

36. Ibid., 265.

37. Corcoran, *Captivity,* 50. Upon his release Michael Corcoran was commissioned a brigadier general commission retroactive to the date of his capture. He was killed on December 22, 1863, near Fairfax Court House, Va. after a drinking spree that ended when his horse fell on him.

CHAPTER 3

1. Patricia L. Faust, ed. *Historical Times Illustrated Encyclopedia of the Civil War* (New York: Harper & Row, 1986), 501–2, hereafter referred to as Faust, *Encyclopedia*.

2. *O.R.,* ser. 1, vol. 13, 402–03.

3. Ibid., ser. 2, vol. 4, 61.

4. Ibid.

5. Ibid., 138.

6. Ibid., 471–72.

7. Ibid., 473 and 539.

8. Ibid., 473.

9. Ibid., 539.

10. Although the execution at Palmyra is the most well-known, eleven POWs were executed by firing squad at Macon City, Missouri three weeks earlier and seventeen were executed at Kirksville, Missouri, the previous August. *O.R.,* ser. 2, vol. 4, 550, 886–87.

11. *O.R.,* ser. 1, vol. 22/1, 817.

12. Griffin Frost, *Camp & Prison Journal* (Quincy, Il.: Quincy Herald Book and Job Office, 1867), 282, hereafter referred to as Frost, *Journal.*

13. The exact details of Allsman's killing were never revealed. His body was never found but a skull believed to be his was located in the area along the creek years later. Henry Clay Dean, *Crimes of the Civil War* (Mt. Pleasant, Iowa: n.p., 1868), 139.

14. *O.R.,* ser. 1, vol. 13, 719. A copy of the order was also hand delivered to Colonel Porter's home in Lewis County, Mo.

15. *O.R.,* ser. 2, vol. 4, 886–87; Richard S. Brownlee, *Gray Ghosts of the Confederacy: Guerrilla Warfare in the West, 1861–1865* (Baton Rouge: Louisiana State University Press, 1958), 88, hereafter referred to as Brownlee, *Gray Ghosts.*

16. Henry C. Dean, "Treatment of Prisoners during the War between the States: Narrative of Henry Clay Dean," *Southern Historical Society Papers* 1, no. 4 (April 1876): 226–28; Stewart Sifakis, *Who Was Who in the Civil War* (New York: Facts on File, 1988), 423, hereafter referred to as Sifakis, *Who Was Who;* Brownlee, *Gray Ghosts,* 82, 88, 89.

17. Palmyra (Mo.) *Courier,* Oct. 20, 1862.

18. Ibid.

19. Frost, *Journal,* 285.

20. Ibid. 286.

21. *O.R.,* ser. 1, vol. 22/1, 818.

22. Palmyra (Mo.) *Courier,* Oct. 20, 1862.

23. Ibid.

24. Ibid.; *O.R.,* ser. 1, vol. 22/1, 818.

25. Palmyra (Mo.) *Courier,* Oct. 20, 1862.

26. These were later claimed by relatives and removed for private burial elsewhere.

27. *New York Times,* Dec. 1, 1862.

28. Ibid.

29. *O.R.,* ser. 2, vol. 4, 946.

30. Ibid., vol. 5, 146.

31. Sifakis, *Who Was Who,* 423; Mark M. Boatner III, *The Civil War Dictionary* (New York: David McKay, 1959), 537–38, hereafter referred to as Boatner, *C.W. Dictionary.*

CHAPTER 4

1. Peggy Robbins, "Hanging Days in Texas." *America's Civil War* 12, no. 2 (May 1999): 52, hereafter referred to as Robbins, "Hanging Days";

Karen Gerhardt, "Reason Dethroned," *North and South* 3, no. 2 (Jan. 2000): 59–60, hereafter referred to as Gerhardt, "Reason Dethroned."

2. George Washington Diamond, "George Washington Diamond's Account of the Great Hanging at Gainesville, 1862," ed. Sam Acheson and Julie Ann Hudson O'Connell, *Southwestern Historical Quarterly* 66, no. 3 (Jan. 1963): 331–335, hereafter referred to as Diamond, "Account"; Richard B. McCaslin, *Tainted Breeze: The Great Hanging at Gainesville, Texas, 1862* (Baton Rouge: Louisiana State University Press, 1994), 12, 15, 31, hereafter referred to as McCaslin, *Tainted Breeze.*

3. James Lemuel Clark, *Civil War Recollections of James Lemuel Clark*, ed. L. D. Clark (College Station: Texas A and M University Press, 1984), 21–22, 76, 103, hereafter referred to as Clark, *Recollections;* Gerhardt, "Reason Dethroned," 66, 63, 61; Robbins, "Hanging Days," 52.

4. McCaslin, *Tainted Breeze,* 205.

5. Thomas Barrett, *The Great Hanging at Gainesville Clark County, Texas, October A.D. 1862* (1885; reprint, Austin: Texas State Historical Association, 1961), 4, hereafter referred to as Barrett, *The Great Hanging.*

6. Ibid.

7. Diamond, "Account," 356–58, 374–78; McCaslin, *Tainted Breeze,* 205.

8. Barrett, *The Great Hanging,* 12.

9. Ibid., 10.

10. Ibid.

11. Ibid., 7.

12. Ibid., 8 and 17. In Barrett's self-serving memoirs he gives the impression he might have been one of the jury's nonslaveholders but according to the 1860 census, Barrett owned one slave (McCaslin, *Tainted Breeze,* 205).

13. Clark, *Recollections,* 107–108.

14. McCaslin, *Tainted Breeze,* 69; Barrett, *The Great Hanging,* 8.

15. Barrett, *The Great Hanging,* 9 and 13.

16. McCaslin, *Tainted Breeze,* 78.

17. Gerhardt, "Reason Dethroned," 63; McCaslin, *Tainted Breeze,* 76–77.

18. Ibid.

19. Barrett, *The Great Hanging,* 11.

20. Ibid., 15.

21. Ibid.

22. Ibid., 16.

23. Ibid., 17.

24. Ibid., 17–18.

25. Clark, *Recollections,* 108.

26. Ibid.

27. Ibid., 112.

28. Barrett, *The Great Hanging,* 18.

29. Ibid., 19–20.

30. McCaslin, *Tainted Breeze,* 52 and 102.

31. Ibid., 86 and 79.

32. Barrett, *The Great Hanging,* 20.

33. Ibid.

34. Ibid., 21.

35. Ibid.; Diamond, "Account," 378; McCaslin, *Tainted Breeze,* 89.

36. *New York Times,* Feb. 25, 1863.

37. Diamond, "Account," 380.

CHAPTER 5

1. *New York Times,* May 29, 1863; *New York Times,* Nov. 25, 1863.

2. Speer, *Portals to Hell,* 108–10.

3. B. T. Morris, "Sixty-Fourth Regiment," *Histories of the Several Regiments and Battalions from North Carolina in the Great War, 1861–'65,* ed. Walter Clark vol. 3 (Goldsboro, N.C.: Nash Brothers, 1901), 661. Hereafter referred to as Morris, "Sixty-Fourth Regiment."

4. Phillip Shaw Paludan, *Victims: A True Story of the Civil War* (Knoxville: University of Tennessee Press, 1981), 32, hereafter referred to as Paludan, *Victims;* Norma D. Morgan, comp., *1860 Federal Census: Madison County, North Carolina* (Pvt. printing, n.p., n.d.) 13, 77, hereafter referred to as Morgan, *1860 Census.* In addition to the two adult slaves (one male and one female) listed in the Keith census schedule, three slave children are also listed.

5. Morris, "Sixty-Fourth Regiment," 659.

6. *O.R.,* ser. 1, vol. 18, 853–54, 856–57; *Memphis Bulletin,* July 15, 1863; *New York Times,* July 24, 1863; Frank Moore, ed., *The Civil War in Song and Story, 1860–1865* (New York: Peter Fenelon Collier, 1882), 206, hereafter referred to as Moore, *The Civil War;* Paludan, *Victims,* 82–83.

7. Ibid.

8. James O. Hall, "The Shelton Laurel Massacre: Murder in the North Carolina Mountains," *Blue and Gray* 8, no. 3 (Feb. 1991): 22, hereafter referred to as Hall, "The Shelton Laurel Massacre"; John C. Inscoe and Gordon B. McKinney, *The Heart of Confederate Appalachia: Western North Carolina in the Civil War* (Chapel Hill: University of North Carolina Press, 2000), 118–19; Matthew Bumgarner, *Kirk's Raiders* (Hickory, N.C.: Piedmont, 2000), 12.

9. Ibid.

10. *O.R.,* ser. 1, vol. 18, 853–54.

11. Ibid.

12. *O.R.,* ser. 1, vol. 15 1/2, 893.

13. *O.R.,* ser. 1, vol. 18, 893; ser. 2, vol. 5, 838–39; Moore, *The Civil War,* 206–7; *Memphis Bulletin,* July 15, 1863; William B. "Bud" Shelton, "The Sheltons and Shelton Laurel, N.C." (manuscript, circa 1960s), 9–11, X.

14. Hall, "The Shelton Laurel Massacre," 22; *Memphis Bulletin,* July 15, 1863, *New York Times,* July 24, 1863; Moore, *The Civil War,* 207; John W. Moore, ed., *Roster of North Carolina Troops in the War between the States,* vol 4 (Raleigh: Ashe and Gatling, 1882), 52, 53, 64, 66, 67, 79; National Archives, RG 109, M270, North Carolina 64th Infantry (11th Battalion), rolls 555, 556, 557, 558. Later research indicates Moore's *Roster* might be in error regarding William Shelton. He might have originally joined the 2nd Battalion NCST on July 4, 1861, and transferred to the 64th at an unrecorded later time, perhaps in July 1862.

15. Morgan, *1860 Census,* 2, 3, 6, 52, 53, 54, 55, 57; National Archives, RG 109, M270, rolls 555, 556, 557, 558. According to these individual roster and military records, it was members of Companies A, C, and D who were on "detached duty by order of H.Q. Dept. of E. Tenn." in Shelton Laurel during this time.

16. *Memphis Bulletin,* July 15, 1863; *New York Times,* July 24, 1863; Moore, *The Civil War,* 206.

17. Ibid.; Shelton family history passed down through generations refers to only thirteen victims. Subsequently it is now the number generally accepted and often published. Contemporary sources, however, including the *O.R.,* refer to a fourteenth victim, originally reported as Joseph Cleandren, later confirmed by his family as being spelled "Clendennon," a fourteen-year-old from nearby Yancey County, who was visiting in the area at the time. His name is included in this work based on those original sources

on the belief that orally passed down family history eventually omitted this victim, because he was unrelated to them and from outside the community.

18. *O.R.,* ser. 1, vol. 18, 893; ser. 2, vol. 5, 838–39; Kenneth C. Wilde, "The Shelton Laurel Massacre, Monday, January 19, 1863," manuscript, 1970, 3; National Archives, RG 109, M270, roll 557, cards 49070464, 49070560, 49070662, 49070754.

19. *O.R.,* ser. 1, vol. 18, 893; ser. 2, vol. 5, 838–39.

20. *O.R.,* ser. 1, vol. 18, 898.

21. Hall, "The Shelton Laurel Massacre," 22–23.

22. Ibid., 23.

23. *Memphis Bulletin,* July 15, 1863; *New York Times,* July 24, 1863; Manly Wade Wellman, *The Kingdom of Madison: A Southern Mountain Fortress and Its People* (Chapel Hill: University of North Carolina Press, 1973), 84–85.

24. *O.R.,* ser. 2, vol. 5, 956.

CHAPTER 6

1. Faust, *Encyclopedia,* 413–14.

2. Ibid.; John S. Bowman, ed., *The Civil War Almanac* (New York: World Almanac Publications, 1983), 55, 57.

3. *O.R.,* ser. 2, vol. 5, 480.

4. Ibid.

5. Ibid., 556, 939; Sifakis, *Who Was Who,* 434.

6. *O.R.,* ser. 2, vol. 5, 556; National Archives, RG 153, MM77, Union Court-Martial and Execution Records. Corbin was born in Campbell County, Kentucky on Mar. 8, 1833. McGraw was born in Harrison County, Kentucky on June 8, 1829.

7. Similar General Orders had been issued in other districts based on the International Rules of War. See General Orders No. 13, Dept. of Missouri, Article 6, issued by Major General Halleck on Dec. 4, 1861; *O.R.,* ser. 2, vol. 1, 234; General Orders No. 11, Army of Virginia (Union), Paragraph III, issued by Major General Pope on July 23, 1862; and Halleck to Thomas, July 1862, *O.R.,* ser. 2, vol. 4, 150.

8. *O.R.,* ser. 2, vol. 5, 556; National Archives, RG 153, MM77.

9. *O.R.,* ser. 2, vol. 5, 556–57. McGraw's middle initial is mistakenly given in the *O.R.* as "G" but according to regiment and family records his

name was Thomas Jefferson McGraw and he actually went by his middle name.

10. *O.R.,* ser. 2, vol. 5, 671–78.

11. National Archives, RG 153, MM77.

12. Speer, *Portals to Hell,* 79, 186; *O.R.,* ser. 2, vol. 8, 990.

13. Ibid. Within thirty days, however, the prison population would climb to over 800 and reach over 1,700 within sixty days.

14. *O.R.,* ser. 2, vol. 5, 544–45.

15. J. C. DeMoss, "Capt. William Francis Corbin," *Confederate Veteran* 5 (1897): 410, hereafter referred to as DeMoss, "William Corbin."

16. Ibid.

17. *Daily Cleveland Herald,* May 16, 1863; Cleveland *Plain Dealer,* May 16, 1863.

18. Ibid.

19. DeMoss, "William Corbin," 410.

20. *Daily Cleveland Herald,* May 16, 1863; *Cleveland Plain Dealer,* May 16, 1863.

21. Ibid.

22. Sandusky (Ohio) *Commercial Register* as reported in the *Daily Cleveland Herald* and the *Cleveland Plain Dealer,* May 16, 1863.

CHAPTER 7

1. *O.R.,* ser. 2, vol. 5, 691.

2. Ibid., 703.

3. Ibid., 691.

4. Ibid., 703.

5. Ibid., 685, 718, 747; vol. 7, 511, 512, 807.

6. Ibid., vol. 5, 710, 718, 961, 963; vol. 6, 19, 719, 751, 752, 757.

7. Ibid., vol. 6, 76, dated July 2, 1863.

8. Ibid., 163, dated July 31, 1863.

9. Ibid., vol. 6, 87; Richmond *Daily Dispatch,* July 7, 1863; *New York Times,* July 11, 1863.

10. *Richmond Daily Dispatch,* July 7, 1863.

11. Ibid.

12. *New York Times,* July 26, 1863.

13. *Richmond Daily Dispatch,* July 7, 1863.

14. *New York Times,* July 26, 1863.

15. George E. Lippincott, "Lee-Sawyer Exchange," *Civil War Times Illustrated* 1, no. 3 (June 1962): 39; *O.R.*, ser. 1, vol. 27/2, 820–21.

16. Ibid., 794.

17. Ibid., ser. 2, vol. 6, 69; Harry E. Neal, "Rebels, Ropes, and Reprieves," *Civil War Times Illustrated* 14, no. 10 (Feb. 1976): 35.

18. Ibid.

19. *O.R.*, ser. 2, vol. 6, 118.

20. *Richmond Daily Dispatch,* July 27, 1863.

21. Robert E. Lee, Jr., *Recollections and Letters of General Robert E. Lee* (New York: Doubleday, 1909), 100, hereafter referred to as Lee, *Letters.*

22. *O.R.*, ser. 2, vol. 6, 76.

23. Neal Dow, *The Reminiscences of Neal Dow: Recollections of Eighty Years* (Portland, Maine: Evening Express, 1898) 730–31, hereafter referred to as Dow, *Reminiscences.*

24. Ibid., 137.

25. *New York Times,* Mar. 8, 1863; *Richmond Daily Examiner,* Oct. 31, 1863.

26. *New York Times,* July 19, 1863. William Henry Fitzhugh Lee, age twenty-six at time of capture and son of Gen. Robert E. Lee, was sometimes referred to as Fitzhugh by family and friends (see Lee, *Letters,* 100–101) but should not be confused with his twenty-eight-year-old cousin Maj. Gen. Fitzhugh Lee. The Chesapeake Hospital was unofficially referred to as McClellan Hospital.

27. James Goldy, "I Have Done Nothing to Deserve This Penalty," *Civil War Times Illustrated* 26, no. 1 (Mar. 1987): 20.

28. *O.R.*, ser. 2, vol. 6, 219.

29. Dow, *Reminiscences,* 730.

30. *O.R.*, ser. 2, vol. 6, 362.

31. Ibid., 358.

32. Ibid., 488.

33. Ibid., 122; ser. 1, vol. 18, 707–708; ser. 1, vol. 25/2, 452; vol. 25/1, 1084.

34. Ibid., ser. 2, vol. 7, 84.

35. Lee, *Letters,* 117.

36. Ibid.

37. Dow, *Reminiscences,* 732.

38. *O.R.*, ser. 2, vol. 6, 927.

39. Ibid., 991.

40. Dow, *Reminiscences, 733.*

41. *O.R.,* ser. 2, vol. 6, 975–76.

42. Dow, *Reminiscences, 733.*

CHAPTER 8

1. Arthur M. Wilcox and Warren Ripley, *The Civil War At Charleston* (Charleston: News and Courier and the Evening Post, 1989), 51; Charles M. Busbee, "Experience of Prisoners under Fire at Morris Island," *Histories of the Several Regiments and Battalions from North Carolina in the Great War, 1861–65,* ed. Walter Clark, vol. 5 (Raleigh: E. M. Uzzell, 1901), 620, hereafter referred to as Busbee, "Experience"; Mauriel P. Joslyn, *Immortal Captives: The Story of 600 Confederate Officers and the United States Prisoner of War Policy* (Shippensburg, Pa.: White Mane, 1996), 17, hereafter referred to as Joslyn, *Immortal Captives.*

2. *O.R.,* ser. 2, vol. 7, 185.

3. Ibid., vol. 6, 124.

4. Ibid., ser. 1, vol. 35/2, 131.

5. Ibid., ser. 2, vol. 6, 128; vol. 7, 185, 217.

6. Ibid., vol. 7, 216–17.

7. *Charleston Mercury,* June 14, 1864.

8. Willard W. Glazier, *The Capture, the Prison Pen, and the Escape: Giving an Account of Prison Life in the South* (Albany: J. Munsell, 1866), 158, hereafter referred to as Glazier, *Capture.*

9. John Azor Kellogg, *Capture and Escape: A Narrative of Army and Prison Life* (Madison: Wisconsin History Comm., 1908), 85–86.

10. Glazier, *Capture,* 158.

11. *O.R.,* ser. 1, vol. 35/2, 132.

12. Ibid., 134.

13. Ibid., vol. 53, 105.

14. Ibid., vol. 35/2, 141.

15. Ibid., ser. 2, vol. 7, 371.

16. Ibid., ser. 1, vol. 35/2, 143.

17. Ibid., 131–32.

18. Joslyn, *Immortal Captives,* 21.

19. Basil W. Duke, *Reminiscences of General Basil W. Duke, C.S.A.* (Garden City, N.Y.: Doubleday, 1911), 368.

20. *O.R.,* ser. 1, vol. 35/2, 163–64.

21. Ibid., 163.

22. Ibid., 163–64. Exchange of commissioned officers had been officially suspended by Secretary Stanton on Dec. 28, 1862. For further details see Speer, *Portals to Hell,* 105.

23. Ibid., 174–75.

24. Ibid., ser. 2, vol. 7, 773, 782.

25. Speer, *Portals to Hell,* 213; *O.R.,* ser. 2, vol. 7, 768.

26. *O.R.,* ser. 2, vol. 7, 567.

27. Isaac W. K. Handy, *United States Bonds; or, Duress by Federal Authority: A Journal of Current Events during an Imprisonment of Fifteen Months at Fort Delaware* (Baltimore: Turnbull Brothers, 1874), 504–5, hereafter referred to as Handy, *Bonds.*

28. John Ogden Murray, *The Immortal Six Hundred: A Story of Cruelty to Confederate Prisoners of War* (Winchester, Va.: Eddy Press, 1905), 29, hereafter referred to as Murray, *Immortal Six Hundred.*

29. Walter G. MacRae, "Confederate Prisoners at Morris Island," *Histories of the Several Regiments and Battalions from North Carolina in the Great War, 1861–'65,* ed. Walter Clark, vol. 4 (Goldsboro, N.C.: Nash Brothers, 1901), 713, hereafter referred to as MacRae, "Morris Island."

30. Handy, *Bonds,* 515.

31. Abram Fulkerson, "The Prison Experience of a Confederate Soldier Who Was under Fire, on Morris Island, from Confederate Batteries," *Southern Historical Society Papers* 22 (Jan.–Dec. 1894): 133, hereafter referred to as Fulkerson, "Prison Experience."

32. *O.R.,* ser. 2, vol. 7, 598.

33. Ibid., 625.

34. Ibid., ser. 1, vol. 35/2, 247.

35. Murray, *Immortal Six Hundred,* 31.

36. Fulkerson, "Prison Experience," 133.

37. Ibid.

38. William H. Morgan, *Personal Reminiscences of the War, 1861–1865* (Lynchburg, Va.: J. Bell, 1911), 233, hereafter referred to as Morgan, *Reminiscences.*

39. John Dunkle [Fritz Fuzzlebug, pseud.], *Prison Life during the Rebellion* (Singer's Glen, Va.: Joseph Funk's Sons, 1869), 20, hereafter referred to as Dunkle, *Prison Life.*

40. George W. Nelson, "Treatment of Prisoners," *Southern Historical Society Papers* 1 (Jan.–June 1876): 249.

41. Fulkerson, "Prison Experience," 134.

42. Ibid., 136.

43. Dunkle, *Prison Life,* 23.

44. Fulkerson, "Prison Experience," 135.

45. MacRae, "Morris Island," 715.

46. Murray, *Immortal Six Hundred,* 92.

47. Busbee, "Experience," 621; Murray, *Immortal Six Hundred,* 93.

48. Murray, *Immortal Six Hundred,* 95.

49. Fulkerson, "Prison Experience," 137; MacRae, "Morris Island," 716.

50. Richard E. Frayser, "Imprisoned under Fire," *Southern Historical Society Papers* 25 (Jan.–Dec. 1897): 370.

51. Francis C. Barnes, "Imprisoned under Fire," *Southern Historical Society Papers* 25 (Jan.–Dec. 1897): 367, hereafter referred to as Barnes, "Imprisoned."

52. Fulkerson, "Prison Experience," 139.

53. Busbee, "Experience," 622.

54. Fulkerson, "Prison Experience," 139.

55. *O.R.,* ser. 2, vol. 7, 783.

56. Murray, *Immortal Six Hundred,* 101.

57. MacRae, "Morris Island," 716.

58. Dunkle, *Prison Life,* 36.

59. Morgan, *Reminiscences,* 238–39.

60. John McElroy, *Andersonville: A Story of Rebel Military Prisons* (Toledo: D. R. Locke, 1879), 518, hereafter referred to as McElroy, *Andersonville.*

61. Murray, *Immortal Six Hundred,* 101.

62. Barnes, "Imprisoned," 367; McElroy, *Andersonville,* 519–20.

63. Speer, *Portals to Hell,* 252.

64. Ibid; Joslyn, *Immortal Captives,* 124.

CHAPTER 9

1. William B. Hesseltine, *Civil War Prisons: A Study in War Psychology* (Columbus: Ohio State University Press, 1930), 43, hereafter referred to as Hesseltine, *Prisons;* Faust, *Encyclopedia,* 616; Speer, *Portals to Hell,* 175, 185, 188.

2. George Levy, *To Die in Chicago: Confederate Prisoners at Camp Dou-*

glas, 1862–1865 (Evanston, Ill.: Evanston, 1994), 52, hereafter referred to as Levy, *To Die;* Thomas A. Head, *Campaigns and Battles of the Sixteenth Regiment Tennessee Volunteers* (Nashville: Cumberland Presbyterian, 1885), 486, hereafter referred to as Head, *Campaigns;* Sparrow Papers, letter of Thomas Sparrow to his wife, dated Dec. 8, 1861, Southern Historical Collection, Manuscripts Department, Wilson Library, University of North Carolina at Chapel Hill.

3. Francis K. Howard, *Fourteen Months in American Bastiles* (Baltimore: Kelly, Hedian, and Piet, 1863), 56, hereafter referred to as Howard, *Fourteen Months;* John Dooley, *John Dooley, Confederate Soldier: His War Journal,* ed. Joseph T. Durkin (Washington: Georgetown University Press, 1945), 138–39.

4. Lawrence Sangston, *Bastiles of the North: By a Member of the Maryland Legislature* (Baltimore: Kelly, Hedian, and Piet, 1863), 63, 71, 78, hereafter referred to as Sangston, *Bastiles;* Howard, *Fourteen Months,* 30; E. A. (Bud) Livingston, "Fort Lafayette," manuscript section from his book, *President Lincoln's Third Largest City: Brooklyn and the Civil War*, 17, hereafter referred to as Livingston, "Fort Lafayette"; Charles E. Frohman, *Rebels on Lake Erie* (Columbus: Ohio Historical Society, 1965), 21; Alonzo Cooper, *In and out of Rebel Prisons* (Oswego, N.Y.: R. J. Oliphant, 1888), 39–40. In addition, Mrs. Wood, wife of the prison commandant Charles O. Wood, became the prison laundress, washing the prisoners' shirts and pants at six cents and ten cents each, respectively (Sangston, *Bastiles,* 63).

5. Sangston, *Bastiles,* 67, 70, 71–72, 78.

6. William H. Knauss, *The Story of Camp Chase* (Nashville: Publishing House of the Methodist Episcopal Church, 1906), 142–43.

7. Ibid., 164, 167.

8. Ibid., 156.

9. *O.R.,* ser. 2, vol. 3, 361; vol. 4, 152–53; vol. 7, 184.

10. Hesseltine, *Prisons,* 43.

11. *O.R.,* ser. 2, vol. 4, 304.

12. Ibid., ser. 2, vol. 5, 367.

13. Ibid.; R. F. Webb, "Prison Life at Johnson's Island," *Histories of the Several Regiments and Battalions from North Carolina in the Great War, 1861–'65,* ed. Walter Clark, vol. 4 (Goldsboro, N.C.: Nash Brothers, 1901), 669, hereafter referred to as Webb, "Prison Life"; J. H. George, "Prisoners at Johnson's Island," *Confederate Veteran* 8 (1900): 442.

14. Bartlett Yancy Malone, *The Diary of Bartlett Yancy Malone,* ed. William Whatley Pierson, Jr. (Chapel Hill: University of North Carolina Press, 1919), 54; Harry Gilmore, *Four Years in the Saddle* (New York: Harper and Brothers, 1866), 289, hereafter referred to as Gilmore, *Four Years.*

15. *O.R.,* ser. 2, vol. 4, 152; James F. Crocker, "Prison Reminiscences," *Southern Historical Society Papers* 34 (Jan.–Dec. 1906): 43–44, hereafter referred to as Crocker, "Prison Reminiscences"; Speer, *Portals to Hell,* 194; Livingston, "Fort Lafayette," 17.

16. Levy, *To Die,* 103; Benjamin Thomas and Harold M. Hyman, *Stanton: The Life and Times of Lincoln's Secretary of War* (New York: Alfred A. Knopf, 1962), 373, hereafter referred to as Thomas and Hyman, *Stanton*; Speer, *Portals to Hell,* 14, 175, 190.

17. Speer, *Portals to Hell,* 175, 190, 194, 317; Levy, *To Die,* 144; *O.R.,* ser. 2, vol. 4, 130–31, 156–57; vol. 6, 1116–17.

18. Levy, *To Die,* 137, 158; Randolph Abbott Shotwell, "The Prison Experiences of Randolph Shotwell," ed. J. G. DeRoulhac Hamilton, *North Carolina Historical Review* 2, no. 2 (April 1925): 158; hereafter referred to as Shotwell, "Prison Experiences"; R. T. Bean, "Seventeen Months in Camp Douglas," *Civil War Quarterly* 20 (Sept. 1987): 15.

19. *O.R.,* ser. 2, vol. 6, 489, 625.

20. Ibid., vol. 8, 993–94; vol. 6, 633.

21. John A. Bateson, "Treatment of Prisoners during the War: Testimony of a Federal Soldier," *Southern Historical Society Papers* 1 (Jan.–June 1876): 293.

22. Frost, *Journal,* 267; Horace Carpenter, "Plain Living at Johnson's Island," *Century Magazine* 41, no. 5 (March 1891): 715.

23. Speer, *Portals to Hell,* 182–83, 184–85, 196, 188, 194.

24. Boatner, *C. W. Dictionary,* 681; *O.R.,* ser. 2, vol. 8, 345; *New York Times,* June 20, 1861.

25. *New York Times,* June 20, 1861.

26. Gilmore, *Four Years,* 290; Thomas D. Witherspoon, "Prison Life at Fort McHenry," *Southern Historical Society Papers* 8 (Apr. 1880): 168.

27. Speer, *Portals to Hell,* 204, 212–13, 262; *Richmond Daily Dispatch* Sept. 28, 1863; Alfred Hoyt Bill, *The Beleaguered City: Richmond, 1861–1865* (New York: Knopf, 1946), 165; Clement Eaton, *A History of*

the Southern Confederacy (New York: Macmillan, 1956), 243; Dow, *Reminiscences,* 721; Richard Heath Dabney, "Prisoners of the Civil War," *Southern Historical Society Papers* 17 (Jan.–Dec. 1889): 380.

28. *O.R.,* ser. 2, vol. 6, 524.

29. Ibid., ser. 2, vol. 7, 150–51, 183–84.

30. Webb, "Prison Life," 669.

31. M. J. Bradley, "The Horrors of Camp Douglas As Related by a Prisoner," ed. Griffin Frost, *Camp and Prison Journal* (Quincy, Ill.: Quincy Herald Book and Job Office, 1867), 267.

32. Crocker, "Prison Reminiscences," 43–44.

33. *New York Times,* Feb. 3, 1864.

34. *O.R.,* ser. 2, vol. 7, 468, 573–74; Henry E. Shepherd, *Narrative of Prison Life at Baltimore and Johnson's Island, Ohio* (Baltimore: Commercial Printing and Stationary, 1917), 15.

35. George H. Moffett, "War Prison Experiences," *Confederate Veteran* 13 (1905): 105, hereafter referred to as Moffett, "War Prison."

36. Crocker, "Prison Reminiscences," 44.

37. W. C. Dodson, "Stories of Prison Life," *Confederate Veteran* 8 (1900): 122.

38. A. W. Sidebottom, "Experiences on Johnson's Island," *Confederate Veteran* 9 (1901): 113.

39. John Allan Wyeth, "Cold Cheer at Camp Morton," *Century Magazine* 41 no. 6 (April 1891): 848.

40. *O.R.,* ser. 2, vol. 8, 997–98.

41. Malachi Bowden, "My Life as a Yankee Captive," ed. Edwin W. Beitzell, *Point Lookout Prison Camp for Confederates* (Leonardtown, Md.: St. Mary's County Historical Society, 1983), 97.

42. Ibid.

43. Shotwell, "Prison Experiences," 337; Levy, *To Die,* 182.

44. J. S. Kimbrough, "Prison Experience," *Confederate Veteran* 22 (1914): 500; Moffett, "War Prison," 108; Randolph Abbott Shotwell, *The Papers of Randolph Abbott Shotwell,* ed. J. G. DeRoulhac Hamilton (Raleigh: North Carolina Historical Commission, 1931), 1:155; C. W. Jones, "In Prison at Point Lookout," ed. Edwin W. Beitzell, *Chronicles of St. Mary's* 11, no. 12 (Dec. 1963): 91–92; Head, *Campaigns,* 477.

45. Crocker, "Prison Reminiscences," 44.

CHAPTER 10

1. Speer, *Portals to Hell,* xiv, xv, 16, 285.

2. Ibid., 288, 291, 292, 293–94; Howell Cobb was also former commandant of the Macon prison, which held Union officer POWs.

3. Jefferson Davis, "The Treatment of Prisoners during the War between the States," *Southern Historical Society Papers* 1, no. 3 (Mar. 1876): 118, hereafter referred to as Davis, "Treatment of Prisoners."

4. Robert E. Lee, "The Treatment of Prisoners during the War between The States," *Southern Historical Society Papers* 1, no. 3 (Mar. 1876): 122.

5. Alexander H. Stephens, *The War between the States,* vol. 2 (Philadelphia: National, 1870), 509.

6. Robert Ould, "The Treatment of Prisoners during the War between The States," *Southern Historical Society Papers* 1, no. 3 (Mar. 1876), 125.

7. Ibid.; Benjamin Franklin Butler, *Butler's Book: Autobiography and Personal Reminiscences of Major-General Benjamin F. Butler* (Boston: A. M. Thayer, 1892), 605, hereafter referred to as Butler, *Butler's Book;* Faust, *Encyclopedia,* 99; Boatner, *C. W. Dictionary,* 109; Sifakis, *Who Was Who,* 96–97; *O.R.,* ser. 2, vol. 6, 845–46, 858.

8. *O.R.,* ser. 2, vol. 5, 795–96; vol. 6, 768.

9. Benjamin F. Butler, "Witness on the Treatment of Prisoners," *Southern Historical Society Papers* 6, no. 4 (Oct. 1878): 187–88, hereafter referred to as Butler, "Treatment of Prisoners"; Butler, *Butler's Book,* 608.

10. Thomas and Hyman, *Stanton,* 373–74, 567; Butler, *Butler's Book,* 610–11; *O.R.,* ser. 2, vol. 7, 575.

11. Butler, *Butler's Book,* 592.

12. Ulysses S. Grant, "The Treatment of Prisoners during the War between the States," *Southern Historical Society Papers* 1, no. 4 (Apr. 1876), 317, hereafter referred to as Grant, "Treatment of Prisoners."

13. Judah Benjamin, "Witness on the Treatment of Prisoners," *Southern Historical Society Papers* 6, no. 4 (Oct. 1878), 186.

14. George L. Christian, "Treatment and Exchange of Prisoners," *Southern Historical Society Papers* 30 (Jan.–Dec. 1902): 81; Davis, "Treatment of Prisoners," 117.

15. John D. Imboden, "The Treatment of Prisoners during the War between the States," *Southern Historical Society Papers* 1, no. 3, (Mar. 1876): 193–95. Besides those at Andersonville Prison, Imboden's other reference was to a contingent of POWs who had been temporarily moved several

miles southwest of the prison to Eufaula, Alabama, in Barbour County, on the Georgia boarder.

16. Butler, "Treatment of Prisoners," 189; Dabney Herndon Maury, "Grant as a Soldier and Civilian," *Southern Historical Society Papers* 5, no. 5 (May 1878): 227, hereafter referred to as Maury, "Grant."

17. Thomas and Hyman, *Stanton*, 374, 567; *O.R.*, ser. 2, vol. 6, 78–79, 92–93; Gideon Welles, *The Diary of Gideon Welles, Secretary of the Navy under Lincoln and Johnson, 1861–1869* (Boston: Houghton Mifflin, 1911), 2: 169–170, hereafter referred to as Welles, *Diary;* Webb Garrison, *The Lincoln No One Knows: The Mysterious Man Who Ran the Civil War* (Nashville: Rutledge Hill, 1993), 123–25; Maury, "Grant," 227. In addition, it was Stanton who not only personally suspended all exchanges of commissioned officers on December 28, 1862, as a result of the Confederate threat to execute all captured Union officers leading black troops into battle, but ordered General Halleck to suspend all further exchanges of enlisted men on May 25, 1863, when the Confederate Congress seemed to continue to back that proposal. Stanton's General Orders No. 207 simply capped off any further possibility of exchanges on parole (Speer, *Portals to Hell,* 105).

18. Ibid.; Grant, "Treatment of Prisoners," 317.

19. Stewart Brooks, *Civil War Medicine* (Springfield, Ill.: Charles C. Thomas, 1966), 67, hereafter referred to as Brooks, *Medicine;* Edward Wellington Boate, "The True Story of Andersonville," *Southern Historical Society Papers* 10 (Jan.–Feb. 1882): 26; L. H. Crawford, "John Yates Beall," *Southern Historical Society Papers* 33 (Jan.–Dec. 1905): 75.

20. Brooks, *Medicine,* 67; Samuel E. Lewis, "An Important Incident," *Southern Historical Society Papers* 30 (Jan.–Dec. 1902): 29; L. M. Park, "The Treatment of Prisoners during the War between the States," *Southern Historical Society Papers* 1, no. 3 (Mar. 1876): 168.

21. Edward Everett Hale, Jr. *William H. Seward* (Philadelphia: George W. Jacobs, 1910), 305–06; Welles, *Diary,* 170; Editors, *The Blockade* (Alexandria, Va.: Time-Life Books, 1983), 12, 14; *O.R.*, ser. 3, vol. 2, 31.

22. *New York Times,* Dec. 27, 1864.

23. Thomas and Hyman, *Stanton,* 371, 373–74, 378.

24. Ibid.; Joslyn, *Immortal Captives,* 12.

25. Frank Freidel, *Francis Lieber: Nineteenth-Century Liberal* (Baton Rouge: Louisiana State University Press, 1948), 307–16, hereafter referred

to as Freidel, *Francis Lieber.*. Sometimes previously referred to in history as the "Articles of War" or the "Principles of War," the English had established articles of war as early as the 1650s and revised and codified them in 1749 for the Royal Navy. Principles for modern ground warfare had been established prior to the Napoleonic era. In fact, Napoléon, himself, referred to Julius Caesar's principles of warfare as being the same as Alexander's and Hannibal's (Charles Andrew Willoughby, *Maneuver in War,* Harrisburg, Pa.: Military Service, 1939, 25, 30; J. F. C. Fuller, *The Foundations of the Science of War,* Fort Leavenworth, Kansas: U.S. Army Command and General Staff College Press, 1993, 209).

26. Freidel, *Francis Lieber,* 309, 318; Thomas and Hyman, *Stanton,* 234.

27. *O.R.,* ser. 2, vol. 5, 671–682.

28. Ibid.; Robert L. Kerby, *Kirby Smith's Confederacy: The Trans-Mississippi South, 1863–1865* (New York: Columbia University Press, 1972), 44–50; *O.R.,* ser. 1, vol. 53, 762.

29. *O.R.,* ser. 1, vol. 43/1, 57–58; vol. 43/2, 202; vol. 44, 13–14.

30. Ibid., vol. 48/1, 237; vol. 22/1, 300, 342.

31. Adolphus E. Richards, *"Richmond Times:* Monument to Mosby's Men," *Southern Historical Society Papers* 27 (Jan.–Dec. 1899) 258.

32. Ibid., 258–59; *O.R.,* ser. 1, vol. 43/1, 566, 811, 822.

33. *O.R.,* ser. 2, vol. 4, 134–35.

34. Ibid.; *Hannibal (Mo.) Herald,* June 10, 1862. Monroe, known as Monroe City today, is on the Marion and Monroe County line.

35. *Quincy (Ill.) Herald,* July 3, 1862; *O.R.,* ser. 2, vol. 4, 233–34.

36. *O.R.,* ser. 2, vol. 4, 232, 236, 328.

37. Ibid., 350, 481, 784, 793, 835, 886–87.

38. Speer, *Portals to Hell,* 2–3; Arthur VanHorn Papers, Library of Congress, Manuscripts Division, David Hall letter to Mary and Arthur Van-Horn, dated Sept. 21, 1861.

39. *New York Times,* Apr. 6, 1863.

40. *O.R.,* ser. 1, vol. 32/2, 279; vol. 44, 14; ser. 2, vol. 5, 691

41. Barrett, *The Great Hanging,* 13.

Bibliography

PRIMARY SOURCES:

Published Material

[Allen, Lawrence M.] *Partisan Campaigns of Col. Lawrence M. Allen.* Raleigh, N.C.: Edwards and Broughton, 1894.

Barnes, F. C. "Imprisoned Under Fire." *Southern Historical Society Papers* 25 (January–December 1897).

Barrett, Thomas. *The Great Hanging at Gainesville, Cooke County, Texas, October, A.D. 1862.* 1885. Reprint, Austin: Texas State Historical Association, 1961.

Barziza, D. U. *Decimus et Ultimus Barziza: The Adventures of a Prisoner of War, 1863–1864.* Edited by R. Henderson Shuffler. Austin: University of Texas Press, 1964. Originally published anonymously in 1865.

Bateson, John A. "Treatment of Prisoners during the War: Testimony of a Federal Soldier." *Southern Historical Society Papers* 1 (Jan.–June 1876).

Bean, R. T. "Seventeen Months in Camp Douglas." *Civil War Quarterly* 20, (September 1987).

Benjamin, Judah P. "Witness on the Treatment of Prisoners." *Southern Historical Society Papers* 6 (July–December 1878).

Boate, Edward Wellington. "The True Story of Andersonville." *Southern Historical Society Papers* 10 (January–February 1882).

Bowden, Malachi. "My Life as a Yankee Captive." Edited by Edwin W. Beitzell. *Point Lookout Prison Camp for Confederates.* Leonardtown, Md.: St. Mary's County Historical Society, 1983.

Boyle, Francis Atherton. "The Prison Diary of Adjutant Francis Atherton Boyle, C.S.A." Edited by Mary Lindsay Thornton. *North Carolina Historical Review* 39, no. 1 (Winter, 1962).

Bradley, M. J. "The Horrors of Camp Douglas As Related by a Prisoner." Edited by Griffin Frost. *Camp and Prison Journal.* Quincy, Ill.: Quincy Herald Book and Job Office, 1867.

Britton, Wiley. *Memoirs of the Rebellion on the Border, 1863.* Chicago: Cushing, Thomas, 1882.

———. *The Civil War on the Border.* New York: G. P. Putnam's Sons, 1890.

Burrows, Rev. J. L. "Recollections of Libby Prison." *Southern Historical Society Papers* 7, nos. 2–3 (February– March 1883).

Busbee, Charles M. "Experience of Prisoners under Fire at Morris Island." *Histories of the Several Regiments and Battalions from North Carolina in the Great War, 1861–65.* Edited by Walter Clark. Vol. 5. Raleigh: E. M. Uzzell, 1901.

Butler, Benjamin F. "Witness on the Treatment of Prisoners." *Southern Historical Society Papers* 6 (July–December 1878).

———. *Butler's Book: Autobiography and Personal Reminiscences of Major-General Benjamin F. Butler.* Boston: A. M. Thaye, 1892.

Caison, Albert Stacey. "Southern Soldiers in Northern Prisons." *Southern Historical Society Papers* 23 (January–December 1895).

Carpenter, Horace. "Plain Living at Johnson's Island." *Century Magazine* 41, no. 5 (March 1891).

Cavada, Frederic F. *Libby Life: Experiences of a Prisoner of War in Richmond, Va., 1863–64.* Philadelphia: King and Baird, 1864.

Christian, George Llewellyn. "Treatment and Exchange of Prisoners." *Southern Historical Society Papers* 30 (January–December 1902).

Clark, James Lemuel. *Civil War Recollections of James Lemuel Clark, Including Previously Unpublished Material on the Great Hanging at Gainesville, Texas, in October 1862.* Edited by L. D. Clark. College Station: Texas A and M University Press, 1984.

Cooper, Alonzo. *In and out of Rebel Prisons.* Oswego, N.Y.: R. J. Oliphant, 1888.

Corcoran, Michael. *The Captivity of General Corcoran: The Only Authentic and Reliable Narrative of the Trials and Suffering Endured during his Twelve Months' Imprisonment in Richmond and Other Southern Cities.* Philadelphia: Barclay, 1865.

Crawford, L. H. "John Yates Beall." *Southern Historical Society Papers* 33 (January–December 1905).

Crocker, James F. "Prison Reminiscences." *Southern Historical Society Papers* 34 (January–December 1906).

Dabney, Richard Heath. "Prisoners of the Civil War." *Southern Historical Society Papers* 17 (January– December 1889).

Davis, Jefferson. "The Treatment of Prisoners during the War between the States." *Southern Historical Society Papers* 1 (January–June 1876).

———. *The Rise and Fall of the Confederate Government.* Vol. 2. New York: D. Appleton, 1881.

Dean, Henry C. "Treatment of Prisoners during the War between the States: Narrative of Henry Clay Dean." *Southern Historical Society Papers* 1, no. 4 (April 1876).

DeMoss, J. C. "Capt. William Francis Corbin." *Confederate Veteran* 5 (1897).

Diamond, George Washington. "George Washington Diamond's Account of the Great Hanging at Gainesville, 1862." Edited by Sam Acheson and Julia Ann Hudson O'Connell. *Southwestern Historical Quarterly* 66, no. 3 (January 1963).

Dodson, W. C. "Stories of Prison Life." *Confederate Veteran* 8 (1900).

Dooley, John. *John Dooley, Confederate Soldier: His War Journal.* Edited by Joseph T. Durkin. Washington: Georgetown University Press, 1945.

Dow, Neal. *The Reminiscences of Neal Dow: Recollections of Eighty Years.* Portland, Maine: Evening Express, 1898.

Duke, Basil W. *History of Morgan's Cavalry.* Cincinnati: Miami Printing, 1867.

———. *Reminiscences of General Basil W. Duke, C.S.A.* Garden City, N.Y.: Doubleday, Page and Co., 1911.

Ellis, Daniel. *Thrilling Adventures of Daniel Ellis: The Great Union Guide of East Tennessee for a Period of Nearly Four Years during the Great Southern Rebellion.* New York: Harper and Brothers, 1867.

Ely, Alfred. *Journal of Alfred Ely: A Prisoner of War in Richmond.* Edited by Charles Lanman. New York: D. Appleton and Company, 1862.

Frayser, Richard E. "Imprisoned under Fire." *Southern Historical Society Papers* 25 (January–December 1897).

Frost, Griffin. *Camp and Prison Journal.* Quincy, Ill.: Quincy Herald Book and Job Office, 1867.

Fulkerson, Abram. "The Prison Experience of a Confederate Soldier Who Was under Fire, on Morris Island, from Confederate Batteries." *Southern Historical Society Papers* 22 (January–December, 1894).

George J. H. "Prisoners at Johnson's Island." *Confederate Veteran* 8 (1900).

George, W. W. "In a Federal Prison." *Southern Historical Society Papers* 29 (January–December, 1901).

Gilmore, Harry. *Four Years in the Saddle.* New York: Harper and Brothers, 1866.

Glazier, Willard W. *The Capture, the Prison Pen, and the Escape: Giving an Account of Prison Life in the South.* Albany: J. Munsell, 1866.

Grant, Ulysses S. "The Treatment of Prisoners during the War between the States." *Southern Historical Society Papers* 1, no. 4 (April 1876).

———. *Personal Memoirs of U. S. Grant.* 2 Vols. New York: Charles L. Webster, 1886.

———. "Exchange of Prisoners." *Southern Historical Society Papers* 17 (January–December 1889).

Hadley, John V. *Seven Months a Prisoner, by "an Indiana Soldier."* Indianapolis: Meikel, 1868.

Hall, William Edward. *Treatise on International Law.* Oxford, England: Clarendon, 1884.

Handy, Isaac W. K. *United States Bonds; or, Duress by Federal Authority: A Journal of Current Events during an Imprisonment of Fifteen Months at Fort Delaware.* Baltimore: Turnbull Brothers, 1874.

Harris, William C. *Prison-Life in the Tobacco Warehouse at Richmond by a Ball's Bluff Prisoner.* Philadelphia: George W. Childs, 1862.

Head, Thomas A. *Campaigns and Battles of the Sixteenth Regiment Tennessee Volunteers.* Nashville: Cumberland Presbyterian, 1885.

Heth, Henry. "The Memoirs of Henry Heth." Edited by James L. Morrison, Jr. Parts 1 and 2. *Civil War History* 8, no. 1 (March 1962): 5–24; 8, no. 3 (September 1962), 300–26.

Hill, Benjamin Harvey. "Exchange of Prisoners." *Southern Historical Society Papers* 17 (January–December 1889).

Hopkins, George. "Imprisoned under Fire." *Southern Historical Society Papers* 25 (January–December, 1897).

Howard, Francis K. *Fourteen Months in American Bastiles.* Baltimore: Kelly, Hedian and Piet, 1863.

Imboden, John D. "The Treatment of Prisoners during the War between the States." *Southern Historical Society Papers* 1 (January–June 1876).

Jeffrey, William H. *Richmond Prisons, 1861–1862.* St. Johnsbury, Vt.: Republican, 1893.

Jones, C. W. "In Prison at Point Lookout." Edited by Edwin W. Beitzell. *Chronicles of St. Mary's* 11, no. 12 (December 1963).

Jones, J. William. *Life and Letters of Robert Edward Lee: Soldier and Man.* New York: Neale, 1906.

———. "The Treatment of Prisoners During the War between the States." *Southern Historical Society Papers* 1 (January–June 1876).

Jones, Samuel. "Letters on the Treatment and Exchange of Prisoners." *Southern Historical Society Papers* 3 (January–June 1877).

Kellogg, John Azor. *Capture and Escape: A Narrative of Army and Prison Life.* Madison: Wisconsin History Commission, 1908.

Kent, James. *Commentaries on American Law.* Vol. I. New York: W. Osborn, 1844.

Kimbrough, J. S. "Prison Experience." *Confederate Veteran* 22 (1914).

Knauss, William H. *The Story of Camp Chase.* Nashville, Tenn.: Publishing House of the Methodist Episcopal Church, 1906.

Lee, Robert E. "The Treatment of Prisoners during the War between the States." *Southern Historical Society Papers* 1 (January–June 1876).

Lee, Robert E., Jr. *Recollections and Letters of General Robert E. Lee.* New York: Doubleday, 1909.

Lewis, Samuel E. "An Important Incident." *Southern Historical Society Papers* 30 (January–December 1902).

MacRae, Walter G. "Confederate Prisoners at Morris Island." *Histories of the Several Regiments And Battalions from North Carolina in the Great War, 1861–'65.* Edited by Walter Clark. Vol. 4. Goldsboro, N.C.: Nash Brothers, 1901.

Malone, Bartlett Yancy. *The Diary of Bartlett Yancy Malone.* Edited by William Whatley Pierson, Jr. Chapel Hill: University of North Carolina Press, 1919.

Maury, Dabney Herndon. "Treatment of Prisoners during the War between the States." *Southern Historical Society Papers* 1 (January–June 1876).

McElroy, John. *Andersonville: A Story of Rebel Military Prisons.* Toledo: D. R. Locke, 1879.

Moffett, George H. "War Prison Experiences." *Confederate Veteran* 13 (1905).

Morgan, William H. *Personal Reminiscences of the War, 1861–1865.* Lynchburg, Va.: J. P. Bell, 1911.

Morris, B. T. "Sixty–Fourth Regiment." *Histories of the Several Regiments And Battalions from North Carolina in the Great War, 1861–'65.* Edited by Walter Clark. Vol. 3. Goldsboro, N.C.: Nash Brothers, 1901.

Mudd, Joseph. *With Porter in North Missouri: A Chapter in the History of the War between the States.* Washington, D.C.: National, 1909.

Murray, John Ogden. *The Immortal Six Hundred: A Story of Cruelty to Confederate Prisoners of War.* Winchester, Va.: Eddy Press, 1905.

Nelson, George W. "Treatment of Prisoners." *Southern Historical Society Papers* 1 (January–June 1876).

Ould, Robert. "The Treatment of Prisoners During the War Between the States." *Southern Historical Society Papers* 1 (January–June 1876).

Park, L. M. "The Treatment of Prisoners during the War between the States." *Southern Historical Society Papers* 1, no. 3 (March 1876).

Rhett, Claudine. "Morris Island." *Southern Historical Society Papers* 12 (July–December 1881).

Richards, Adolphus E. "*Richmond Times:* Monument of Mosby's Men." *Southern Historical Society Papers* 27 (January–December 1899).

Rodgers, Ruth. "Prisoners of War, North and South." *Southern Historical Society Papers* 34 (January–December 1906).

Sangston, Lawrence. *Bastiles of the North: By a Member of the Maryland Legislature.* Baltimore: Kelly, Hedian, and Piet, 1863.

Schofield, John M. *Forty-six Years in the Army.* New York: Century, 1897.

Shepherd, Henry E. *Narrative of Prison Life at Baltimore and Johnson's Island, Ohio.* Baltimore: Commercial Printing and Stationary, 1917.

Sheridan, Philip H. *Personal Memoirs of P. H. Sheridan.* 2 Vols. New York: Charles L. Webster, 1888.

Sherrill, Miles O. *A Soldier's Story: Prison Life and Other Incidents in the War of 1861–'65.* Raleigh: n.p., 1911.

Shotwell, Randolph Abbott. "The Prison Experiences of Randolph Shotwell." Edited by J. G. DeRoulhac Hamilton. *North Carolina Historical Review* 2, no. 2 (April 1925).

———. *The Papers of Randolph Abbott Shotwell.* Edited by J. G. DeRoulhac Hamilton. 3 vols. Raleigh: North Carolina Historical Commission, 1931.

Sidebottom, A. W. "Experiences on Johnson's Island." *Confederate Veteran* 9 (1901).

Stephens, Alexander H. *The War between the States.* Vol. 2. Philadelphia: National, 1870.

———. "Treatment of Prisoners." *Southern Historical Society Papers* 1, (January–June 1876).

U.S. War Department. *War of the Rebellion: A Compilation of the Official Records of the Union and Confederate Armies.* 128 Vols. Washington, D.C.: General Printing Office, 1880–1901.

Webb, R. F. "Prison Life at Johnson's Island." *Histories of the Several Regiments and Battalions from North Carolina in the Great War, 1861–'65.* Edited by Walter Clark. Vol. 4. Goldsboro, N.C.: Nash Brothers, 1901.

Welles, Gideon. *The Diary of Gideon Welles, Secretary of the Navy under Lincoln and Johnson, 1861–1869.* Vol. 2. Boston: Houghton Mifflin, 1911.

Wheaton, Henry. *Elements of International Law: With a Sketch of the History of the Science.* Philadelphia: Carey, Lea, and Blanchard, 1836.

Williams, R. H. *With the Border Ruffians: Memories of the Far West, 1852–1868.* Edited by E. W. Williams. Toronto: Musson Book, 1919.

Witherspoon, Thomas D. "Prison Life at Fort McHenry." *Southern Historical Society Papers* 8, no. 2 (February, 1880).

Wright, Henry H. "'The Awfulest Time I Ever Seen': A Letter From Sherman's Army." Edited by Howard Norman Monnett. *Civil War History* 8, no. 3 (September 1962): 283–289.

Wyeth, John Allan. "Cold Cheer at Camp Morton." *Century Magazine* 41, no. 6 (April 1891).

———. "Prisoners, North and South." *Southern Historical Society Papers* 19 (January–December 1891).

Newspapers

Army and Navy Journal
Asheville (N.C.) *Citizen-Times*
Asheville (N.C.) *News*
Asheville (N.C.) *Times*
Carrollton (Ky.) *Democrat*
Charleston *Mercury*
Cleveland *Plain Dealer*
Daily Cleveland Herald
Frank Leslie's Illustrated Newspaper
Hannibal (Mo.) *Courier-Post*
Hannibal (Mo.) *Herald*
Harper's Monthly
Harper's Weekly
Houston Telegraph
London Star
Marshall (N.C.) *News-Record and Sentinel*
Memphis Bulletin
Memphis *Daily*
New York Herald
New York Times
Palmyra (Mo.) *Courier*
Raleigh *News and Observer*
Raleigh *North Carolina Standard*
Richmond *Daily Dispatch*
Richmond *Daily Examiner*
San Antonio *Herald*
Sandusky (Ohio) *Commercial Register*
St. Louis *Daily Democrat*
St. Louis *Globe*
St. Louis *Post-Dispatch*
Washington (D.C.) Daily National Intelligencer
Westliche Post

Unpublished Material

Beck, Dorris Dills. "Five Dills Brothers in Civil War." Genealogical manu-
    script, along with accumulated war, service, and POW records of five
    brothers all serving in Co. H, 62nd North Carolina Infantry and all

taken prisoner at Cumberland Gap, September 9, 1863. One was in-carcerated at Johnson's Is. Prison and the other four at Camp Douglas.

Beck-Buchanan Family Papers. Accumulated war and service records of four Buchanan brothers serving together in Co. B, 25th North Carolina Regiment.

Burnett, Lynn. Genealogical information, including accumulated war, service, and POW records of Lt. Marion Francis Corbin, Co. B, 4th Kentucky Cavalry, along with other official documents, records, and letters regarding the Corbin family of Kentucky.

Deyton, Jason B. "History of Toe River Valley to 1865." Bound typed manuscript. Pvt. Printed, circa 1930s.

Franklin, Nancy Norton. Pension Deposition and Affidavit No. 176.751.

————. General Affidavit. No. 176.751.

Freeman, M. O., comp. "The Civil War Diary of Henry Freeman." Bound typed manuscript. Pvt. Printed, 1978.

Kirk, George W. Pension Deposition and Affidavits. Nos. 286.396, 571.150, 595.334, and 929.318.

Kirk, Leon. "George Kirk and the Civil War." Genealogical manuscript and Civil War military history compiled and written by his great grandnephew.

————. "Capt. John L. Kirk . . ." Genealogical manuscript and Civil War military history compiled and written by his great-grandson.

Livingston, E. A. (Bud). "Fort Lafayette." Manuscript section from his book, *President Lincoln's Third Largest City: Brooklyn and the Civil War.*

Moore, Nancy. Pension Depositon and Affidavit, Mother's Dependence, No. 176.769.

Norton, George. Deposition to case No. 176.751. Three handwritten pages dated October 4, 1883.

Shelton, William B. "Bud." "The Sheltons and Shelton Laurel, N.C." Manuscript, circa 1960s.

Slagle, Dan, comp. "Dr. James A. Keith, 1824–1895." Typed manuscript, 1998.

Walter, John F., comp. "Second North Carolina (US) Mounted Infantry."

White, H. A. Affidavit to case No. 176.751. One handwritten page dated March 3, 1885.

Wilde, Kenneth C. "The Shelton Laurel Massacre, Monday, January 19, 1863." Manuscript, 1970. Researched and written by a former resident of Madison County, North Carolina, who claims relationship to a number of victims as well as some of the executioners. Rendition contains more genealogical information about the victims than is generally seen in other accounts, substantiated by other individual genealogical sources and census records.

National Archives, Washington, D.C.
RG 94, M594, 1st Tennessee (Union) Cavalry. Roll 188.
RG 94, M594, 2nd North Carolina (Union) Mounted Infantry, 3rd North Carolina (Union) Mounted Infantry. Roll 139.
RG 109, Ch. 2, Vol. 207 1/2.
RG 109, Ch. 8, Vol. 91 1/2, Parts 7, 8, 9. Record book of 1st Military District, Missouri State Guard.
RG 109, M230, Index, North Carolina Confederate Troops.
RG 109, M270, North Carolina 64th Infantry (11th Battalion). Rolls 555, 556, 557, 558.
RG 109, M322, 2nd Missouri (Confederate) Cavalry. Rolls 17, 20.
RG 109, M322, 3rd Missouri (Confederate) Cavalry. Rolls 22, 25.
RG 109, M380, Index, Missouri Confederate Troops.
RG 109, M390, Index, Missouri Union Troops.
RG 109, M405, 3rd Missouri (Union) State Militia. Rolls 79, 82, 85, 86, 92.
RG 109, M405, 47th Missouri Infantry. Roll 801.
RG 153, MM77, Union Court-Martial and Execution Records.
RG 249, E7, Vols. 1–5. Miscellaneous correspondence from the U.S. Adjutant and Inspector General's Office regarding prisoners of war held by the C.S.A.

Library of Congress, Manuscript Division, Washington, D.C.
Bradbury, William H. Papers.
Buford, Charles. Papers.
Davis, Jefferson. Papers.
Grant, Ulysses Simpson. Papers.
Herndon, William Henry. Papers.
Hills, William G. Papers.
Hitchcock, Ethan Allen. Papers.
Larned, Daniel Read. Papers.
Lee, Robert Edward. Papers.

Lincoln, Abraham. Papers.

Mangum, Willie Person. Papers.

Montgomery Family. Papers.

Mosby, John Singleton. Papers.

Stanton, Edwin McMasters. Papers.

Steiner, Walter Ralph. Papers.

Stuart, George Hay. Papers.

Underwood, John Curtis. Papers.

VanHorn, Arthur. Papers.

**Southern Historical Collection, Manuscripts Department, Wilson
Library, University of North Carolina at Chapel Hill.**

Blanchard Family. Papers.

Colston, Raleigh E. Papers.

Fortescue, Louis. Papers and Diary.

Gray, Charles C. Papers and Diary.

Kean, Augustus C. Papers.

McMichael, James R. Papers and Diary.

Olmstead, Charles H. Papers.

Richardson, Harry B. Papers.

Sparrow, Thomas. Papers and Diary.

Wallace, James T. Diary.

SECONDARY SOURCES:

Alotta, Robert I. *Civil War Justice: Union Army Executions under Lincoln.*
Shippensburg, Pa.: White Mane, 1989.

America's Civil War, 1, no. 1 to 14, no. 3. (May 1988 to July 2001).

Bailey, Lloyd. "George Washington Kirk: Hero or Villain?" *The Toe River
Valley Historical Book.* Burnsville, N.C.: Yancey Graphics, 1983.

Baker, Charles Estell. "The Palmyra Massacre." *Confederate Veteran* 36,
no.1 (January–February 1988).

Bill, Alfred Hoyt. *The Beleaguered City: Richmond, 1861–1865.* New York:
Knopf, 1946.

Blanton, B. F. "A True Story of the Border Wars." *Missouri Historical Review* 17, no. 1 (October 1922).

Boatner, Mark M., III. *The Civil War Dictionary.* New York: David
McKay, 1959.

Bowman, John S., ed. *The Civil War Almanac.* New York: World Almanac, 1983.

Brooks, Stewart. *Civil War Medicine.* Springfield, Ill.: Charles C. Thomas, 1966.

Brownlee, Richard S. *Gray Ghosts of the Confederacy: Guerrilla Warfare in the West, 1861–1865.* Baton Rouge: Louisiana State University Press, 1958.

————. *The Battle of Pilot Knob.* Iron County, Mo.: Missouri Civil War Centennial Commission, 1964.

Bumgarner, Matthew. *Kirk's Raiders.* Hickory, N.C.: Piedmont Press, 2000.

Civil War History, 7, no. 4 to 10, no. 2 (December 1961 to June 1964).

Civil War Times Illustrated, 1, no. 1 to 40, no. 4 (April 1962 to Aug. 2001).

Clark, Walter, ed. *Histories of the Several Regiments and Battalions from North Carolina in the Great War 1861–'65.* 5 vols. Goldsboro and Raleigh: Nash Brothers and E. M. Uzzell, 1901.

Collins, Michael. *Cooke County, Texas: Where the South and West Meet.* Gainesville, Tex.: Cooke County Heritage Society, 1981.

Dean, Henry Clay. *Crimes of the Civil War.* Mt. Pleasant, Iowa: n.p., 1868.

Dyer, Frederick H. *A Compendium of the War of the Rebellion.* 3 vols. Des Moines: Dyer Publishing, 1908.

Eaton, Clement. *A History of the Southern Confederacy.* New York: Macmillan, 1956.

Editors. *The Blockade.* Alexandria, Va.: Time-Life Books, 1983.

Edwards, John N. *Shelby and His Men; or the War in the West.* Cincinnati: Miami Printing, 1867.

Evans, Clement A., ed. *Confederate Military History.* Vol. 9. Atlanta: Confederate, 1899.

Facts About Jefferson Barracks National Cemetery. St. Louis: n.p., 1989.

Faust, Patricia L., ed. *Historical Times Illustrated Encyclopedia of the Civil War.* New York: Harper and Row, 1986.

Fehrenbacher, Don E., and Virginia Fehrenbacher, comps. and eds. *Recollected Words of Abraham Lincoln.* Stanford, Calif.: Stanford University Press, 1996.

Fellman, Michael. *Inside War: The Guerrilla Conflict in Missouri during the American Civil War.* New York: Oxford University Press, 1989.

Ford, Annette Gee, comp. and ed. *The Captive: Major John H. Gee, Commandant of the Confederate Prison at Salisbury, North Carolina, 1864–1865. A Biographical Sketch with Complete Court-Martial Transcript.* Salt Lake City, Utah: Utah Bookbinding, 2000.

Fox, William F. *Regimental Losses in the American Civil War, 1861–1865.* Albany: Joseph McDonough, 1898.

Freidel, Frank. *Francis Lieber: Nineteenth-Century Liberal.* Baton Rouge: Louisiana State University Press, 1948.

Frohman, Charles E. *Rebels on Lake Erie.* Columbus: Ohio Historical Society, 1965.

Fuller, J. F. C. *The Foundations of the Science of War.* Fort Leavenworth, Kans.: U.S. Army Command and General Staff College Press, 1993.

Garrison, Webb. *The Lincoln No One Knows: The Mysterious Man Who Ran The Civil War.* Nashville, Tenn.: Rutledge Hill, 1993.

Gaston, A. P. *Partisan Campaigns of Col. Lawrence M. Allen, Commanding the 64th Regiment, North Carolina State Troops, during the Late Civil War.* Raleigh, N.C.: Edwards and Broughton, 1894.

Gerhardt, Karen. "Reason Dethroned." *North & South* 3, no. 2 (January 2000).

Goldy, James. "I Have Done Nothing to Deserve This Penalty." *Civil War Times Illustrated* 26, no. 1 (March 1987).

Goodrich, Thomas. *Black Flag: Guerrilla Warfare on the Western Border, 1861–1865.* Bloomington: Indiana University Press, 1995.

Goodspeed, comp. *Goodspeed's History of Southeast Missouri.* n.p: Goodspeed, 1888.

———, comp. *Goodspeed's History of Greene County, Tennessee.* n.p.: Goodspeed, 1887.

Gunter, Pete A. Y. "The Great Gainesville Hanging, October, 1862: Rebel Colonel Bourland's 'Witch Hunt' in North Texas." *Blue & Gray Magazine* 3, no. 5 (April–May, 1986).

Hale, Edward Everett, Jr. *William H. Seward.* Philadelphia: George W. Jacobs, 1910.

Hall, James O. "The Shelton Laurel Massacre: Murder in the North Carolina Mountains." *Blue and Gray* 8, no. 3 (February 1991).

Hesseltine, William B. *Civil War Prisons: A Study in War Psychology.* Columbus: Ohio State University Press, 1930.

Holzer, Harold, comp. and ed. *Dear Mr. Lincoln: Letters to the President.* Reading, Mass.: Addison-Wesley, 1993.

Ingenthron, Elmo. *Borderland Rebellion.* Branson, Mo.: Ozark Mountain, 1980.

Inscoe, John C., and Gordon B. McKinney. *The Heart of Confederate Appalachia: Western North Carolina in the Civil War.* Chapel Hill: University of North Carolina Press, 2000.

Joslyn, Mauriel P. *Immortal Captives: The Story of 600 Confederate Officers and the United States Prisoner of War Policy.* Shippensburg, Pa.: White Mane, 1996.

———. *The Biographical Roster of the Immortal 600.* Shippensburg, Pa.: White Mane, 1992.

Kerby, Robert L. *Kirby Smith's Confederacy: The Trans-Mississippi South, 1863–1865.* New York: Columbia University Press, 1972.

Keys, Thomas Bland. *The Uncivil War: Union Army and Navy Excesses in the Official Records.* Biloxi, Miss.: Beauvoir, 1991.

LeGrand, Louis. *The Military Hand-Book and Soldier's Manual of Information Including the Official Articles of War.* New York: Beadle, 1861.

Levy, George. *To Die in Chicago: Confederate Prisoners at Camp Douglas, 1862–1865.* Evanston, Ill.: Evanston, 1994.

Lippincott, George E. "Lee-Sawyer Exchange." *Civil War Times Illustrated* 1, no. 3 (June 1962).

Long, Roger. "The General's Tour—Johnson's Island Prison: 'Hell Has Torments of Cold.'" Part I. *Blue and Gray Magazine* 4, no. 4 (February–March 1987).

Lonn, Ella. *Desertion during the Civil War.* New York: Century, 1928.

———. *Salt as a Factor in the Confederacy.* New York: W. Neale, 1933.

Lowry. Thomas P. *Don't Shoot That Boy! Abraham Lincoln and Military Justice.* Mason City, Iowa: Savas, 1999.

Madison County Heritage Book Committee. *Madison County Heritage North Carolina.* Vol. 1. Waynesville, N.C.: Don Mills, 1994.

McCaffrey, James M. "The Palmyra Massacre." *Civil War Times Illustrated* 19, no. 8 (December 1980).

McCaslin, Righard B. *Tainted Breeze: The Great Hanging at Gainesville, Texas, 1862.* Baton Rouge: Louisiana State University Press, 1994.

McElroy, John. *The Struggle for Missouri.* Washington, D.C.: National Tribune, 1909.

McKinney, Gordon B. "Women's Role in Civil War Western North Carolina." *North Carolina Historical Review* 69, no. 1 (January 1992): 42–45.

McLeod, John Angus. *From These Stones: Mars Hill College, the First Hundred Years.* Mars Hill, N.C.: Mars Hill College, 1955.

Monaghan, Jay. *Civil War on the Western Border, 1854–1865.* New York: Bonanza Books, 1955.

Moore, Frank, ed. *The Civil War in Song and Story, 1860–1865.* New York: Peter Fenelon Collier, 1882.

Moore, John W., ed. *Roster of North Carolina Troops in the War between the States.* 4 vols. Raleigh: Ashe and Gatling, 1882.

Morgan, Norma D., comp. *1860 Federal Census: Madison County, North Carolina.* Pvt. print., n.p., n.d.

Neal, Harry E. "Rebels, Ropes, and Reprieves." *Civil War Times Illustrated* 14, no. 10 (February 1976).

Paludan, Phillip Shaw. *Victims: A True Story of the Civil War.* Knoxville: University of Tennessee Press, 1981.

Parrish, William F. "The Palmyra 'Massacre': A Tragedy of Guerrilla Warfare." *Journal of Confederate History* 1 (fall 1988).

Peeke, Hewson L. "Johnson's Island." *Ohio Archaeological and Historical Publications,* vol. 26. Columbus: Fred R. Heer, 1918.

Peterson, Cyrus A. *Narrative of the Capture and Murder of Major James Wilson.* St. Louis: A. R. Fleming, 1906.

Robbins, Peggy. "Hanging Days in Texas." *America's Civil War* 12, no. 2 (May 1999).

Shoemaker, Floyd C. "The Story of the Civil War in Northeast Missouri." *Missouri Historical Review* 7, no. 3 (April 1913)

Sifakis, Stewart. *Who Was Who in the Civil War.* New York: Facts on File, 1988.

Siler, Leon M. "My Lai Controversy Recalls 1863 Tragedy on the Shelton Laurel," *State* 37, no. 17 (February 1, 1970).

Smallwood, James. "Disaffection in Confederate Texas: The Great Hanging at Gainesville." *Civil War* 22 (December 1976).

Southern Historical Society Papers. 52 Vols. Richmond: Southern Historical Society, 1876–1959.

Speer, Lonnie R. *Portals to Hell: Military Prisons of the Civil War.* Mechanicsburg, Pa.: Stackpole Books, 1997.

Suderow, Bruce, ed. "We Did Not Take Any Prisoners." *Civil War Times Illustrated* 23, no. 3 (May 1984).

Tennessee Civil War Centennial Commission. *Tennesseans in the Civil War: A Military History of the Confederate and Union Units with Available Rosters of Personnel.* 2 Vols. Nashville: Civil War Centennial Commission, 1964.

Thomas, Benjamin P., and Harold M. Hyman. *Stanton: The Life and Times of Lincoln's Secretary of War.* New York: Knopf, 1962.

Thomas, Emory M. *Robert E. Lee: A Biography.* New York: Norton, 1995.

Union Historical Company, comp. *History of Jackson County, Missouri.* Birdsall, Mo.: Williams, 1881.

Wellman, Manly Wade. *The Kingdom of Madison: A Southern Mountain Fastness and Its People.* Chapel Hill: University of North Carolina Press, 1973.

———. "With Your Teeth in a Throat!" Raleigh *News and Observer,* November 18, 1956.

Wilcox, Arthur M., and Warren Ripley. *The Civil War at Charleston.* Charleston: News And Courier and the Evening Post, 1989.

Willoughby, Charles Andrew. *Maneuver in War.* Harrisburg, Pa.: Military Service, 1939.

Winter, Nevin O. *A History of Northwest Ohio.* Chicago: Lewis, 1917.

Winter, William C. *The Civil War in St. Louis: A Guided Tour.* St. Louis: Missouri Historical Society, 1994.

Index

185